Renovating Prints, Paintings and Frames

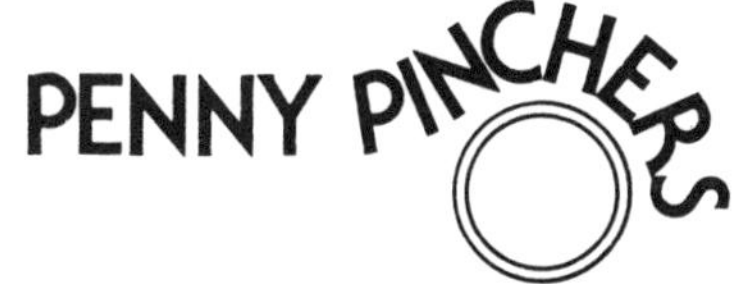

Contents

Introduction

The renovation of old paintings is a subject in which more and more people are becoming interested. This is especially so with the do-it-yourself trend of recent years, and whereas not everyone may wish to be an expert restorer, anyone who owns a painting or print, either purchased or inherited, will profit from an understanding of the basic mechanics of 'picture science'. As expertise becomes more expensive and preservation and conservation of existing raw materials becomes more necessary, then renovation by the amateur is made increasingly relevant. In the case of frames, always expensive items, renovation is certainly worthwhile, not only to save cost, but also to preserve the aesthetic, period look of the complete picture.

Due to the lack of skilled restorers, most renovation work done on watercolours and prints until fairly recently was in fact undertaken by the collectors themselves – sometimes, admittedly, to the picture's detriment. The advice contained in this book should help the would-be renovator by explaining some of the techniques available to the experts, and also some of the inherent dangers to be avoided. Of course where valuable works of art are concerned, one has to be careful that, by trying to be a penny-pincher, one does not in fact become a pound-loser. Amongst the less important art auction sales of the major salerooms appear many works damaged to a greater or lesser degree, sometimes merely dirty, but often scarred due to over-zealous or unskilled restoration work. In these cases of course, the eventual prices realised are far below what they would have reached if in better condition.

Since old paintings and prints are becoming more sought after, even lesser items can be of much greater value than was expected. So if you are fortunate enough to own a painting or print of value, or even if you only think you may own one, by all means learn the techniques contained in this book but before embarking on an extensive renovation, obtain an expert's advice and if necessary leave the restoration work to him. On the other hand, if all you want is an improvement in the appearance of a favourite picture by Aunt Matilda and the picture or frame is due to be thrown away, then you have nothing to lose at all in any experimental renovation work.

Remember that, despite attentions from would-be restorers, wars, riots, pollution and other hazards, innumerable seemingly fragile paintings and prints have survived as reminders of previous ages and as such are not only furnishings but can be viewed as parts of each one's own inheritance, to be lived with and enjoyed now and in the future.

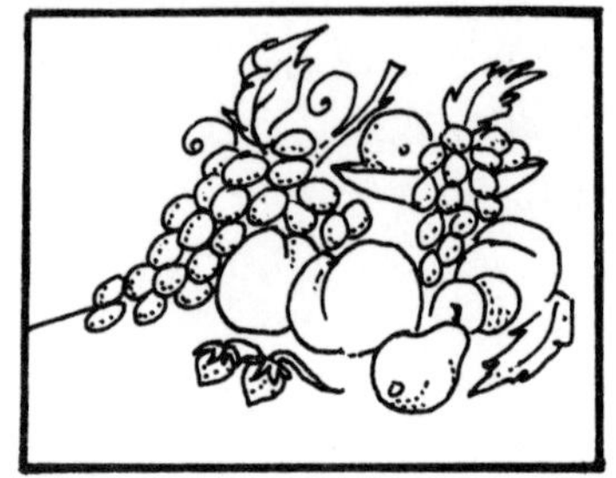

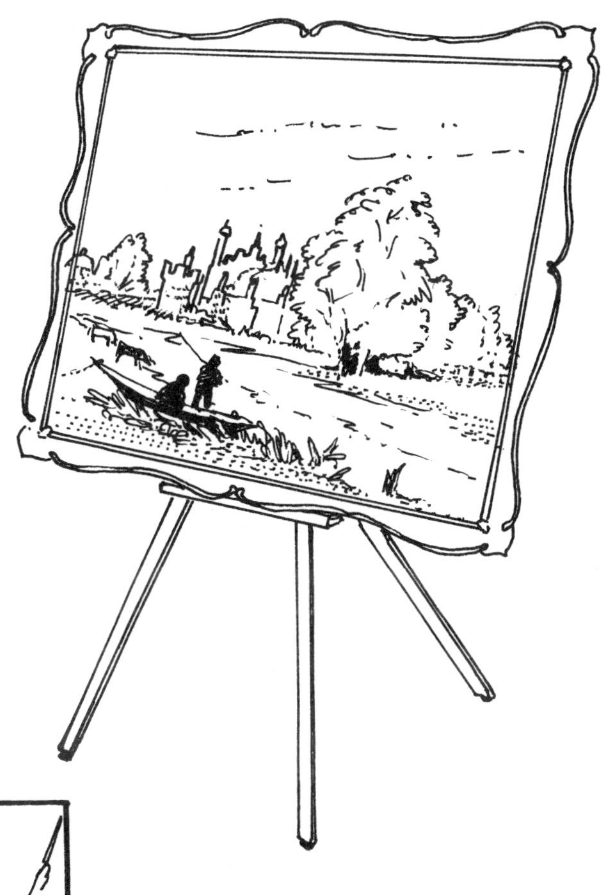

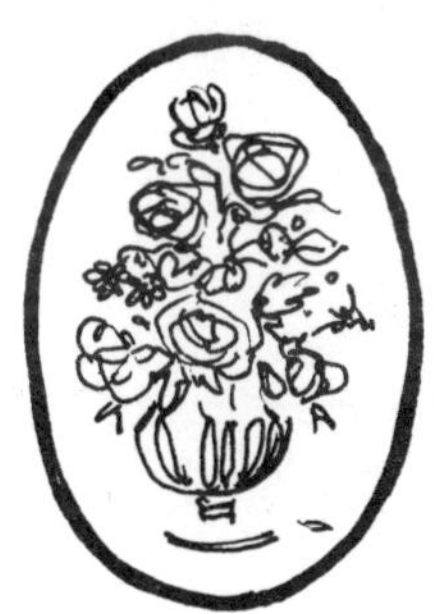

Some examples of different types of paintings

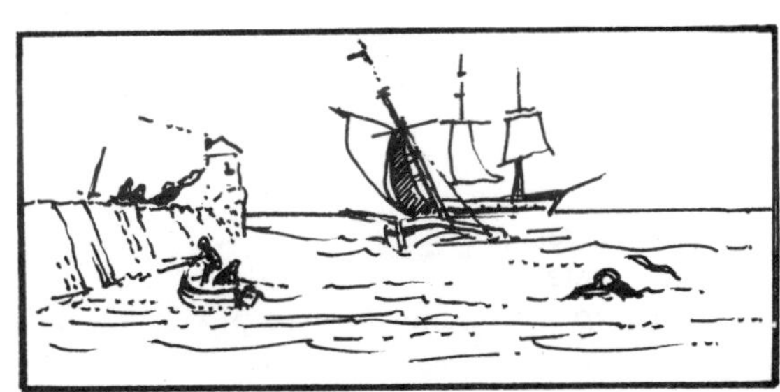

Oil paintings

Dark surfaces

Rows of dark oil paintings set in baronial halls have led many people to believe that the majority of old paintings are boring and dull. However one must bear in mind that sometimes these paintings are presenting themselves to us with the accretions of not just a few years but perhaps the dust and grime of three hundred years or more. Any housewife knows how dust accumulates in even the most inaccessible and protected of places, and whereas electric light and central heating are relative newcomers, the wax candle and open fire which produce their own brand of dust, dirt and discoloration have been leaving slight deposits on a room's furnishings for many years. The windows, glass, furniture, floors and cutlery have all been cleaned many times over, but how does one clean that old picture over the fireplace? Through quite rightly not wishing to cause damage, people leave these relics – sometimes survivors of the cavalier or puritan age – to look darker and darker.

A further complication in this darkening process is due to the fact that almost all old paintings have been coated with a varnish made from a mastic resin. This varnish looked fine when first brushed on, but it gradually turns yellow and after many years it becomes completely brown. Added to this, heavy cigarette or tobacco smoking in a room over many years adds a further brown layer of nicotine deposits, so it is not surprising that a good many paintings originally executed in quite brilliant colours now appear as dull,

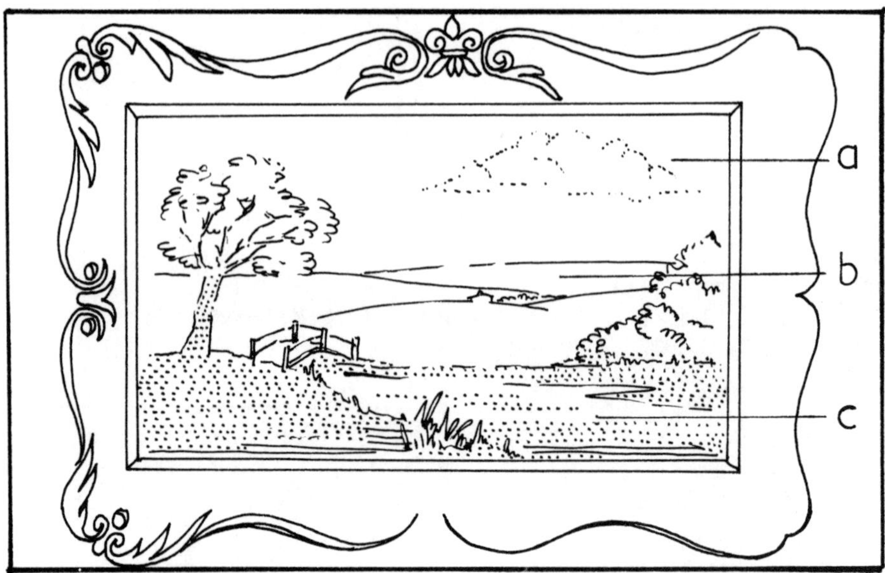

Features of the darkening process: a. the sky appears yellow; b. the distance appears dark green; c. the foreground appears dark brown

unattractive shadows of their former selves. Typical changes in appearance are that the browns, greens and reds appear almost black, whites show as dirty, brownish yellow and blues appear as dull greens.

However, it must also be stated that sometimes owners think that their paintings are dirtier than they actually are. For example, many painters of the eighteenth and early nineteenth centuries had a great fondness for brown, such that their landscapes often have a great deal of brown detail in the foreground. When originally painted and varnished, this would have contrasted nicely with the landscape vista in the distance and was accepted as part of the recognised formula for successfully constructing a presentable painting. Most portrait painters gave a dark background to the sitter, and in still-life paintings too a dark background was used as a contrast against the details of flowers or fruit. It is in these cases that one can sometimes come to the wrong conclusion and think that the painting is dirty, when in fact the picture was originally intended that way. Any attempt at cleaning such a painting would give very little result, with the temptation to try and clean in a harder, more vigorous way finally resulting in a badly damaged painting with a rubbed paint surface.

Sometimes earlier attempts at cleaning or renovation only reveal themselves in the years that follow. For example, many old oil paintings have had linseed oil or other oils rubbed on them. These oils discolour and leave a sticky surface for more dust and dirt to settle on.

All these factors contribute to the appearance of your pictures. While this may make the thought of successful cleaning daunting for the amateur, it is wise to know the mechanics of picture darkening and not to be too hasty in pronouncing a picture 'dirty'.

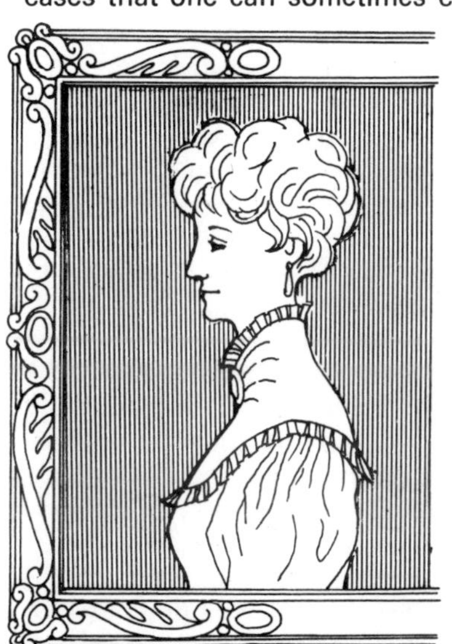

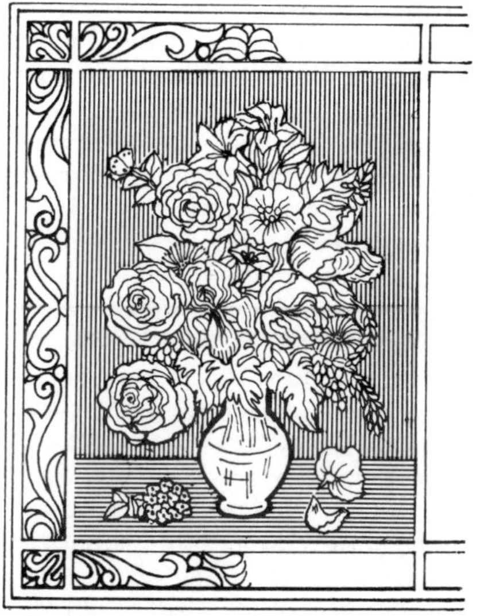

Examples of dark backgrounds in a portrait and a still-life

Oil paintings

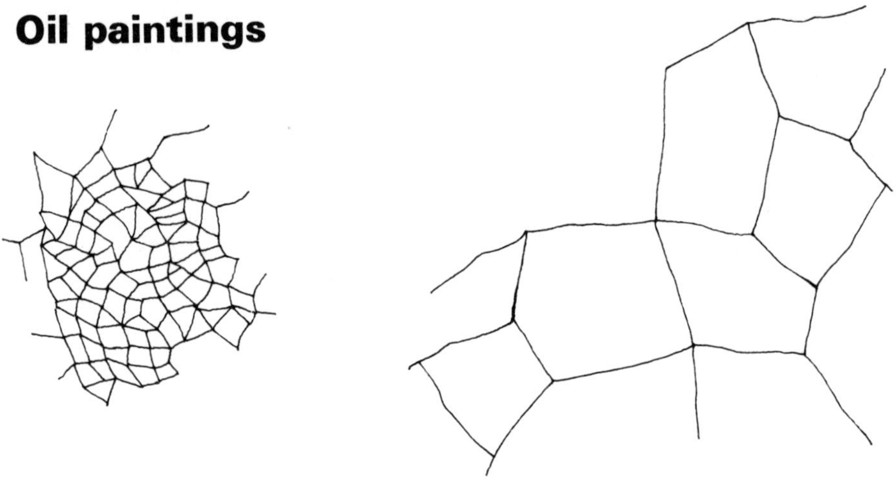

The appearance of the craquelure often enables an expert to place a date on a painting

Surface cracks

Cracks in paint, known as the 'craquelure', are to pictures what a patina is to old bronze – in fact, they are becoming considered a hallmark of antiquity. Oil paint hardens with time so that a hundred-year-old oil painting painted on canvas, shows cracks over its surface approximately 1–1½in apart. As the age increases more cracks appear such that a seventeenth-century painting appears covered in a fine cobweb pattern of cracks sometimes only ¼in apart. The appearance of the craquelure allows an expert to place a date on the painting, often, after considering other factors, to within a few years.

However, various other factors can influence the degree of cracking. Often the stretcher (the wooden frame which has the canvas tacked over it) shows through in the pattern of the cracks. On some eighteenth- and nineteenth-century paintings there appear rings of cracks which, some have reasoned, may arise from the artist's habit of resting a painting-stick against the canvas during the painting. Cracks which are dispersed evenly throughout the paint film are not to be worried about, but are a feature to be proud of. In fact, the time to worry about the cracks is when they are not in evidence; the art-dealing experts viewing a picture sale are looking specifically for areas in a painting where no cracks appear. This is because if an old painting has been restored (ie repainted over a damaged area), cracks in new paint cannot be easily manufactured and the restoration becomes obvious to a trained eye. Of course this is not the complete guide to spotting restored areas, as some skilful restorers can complete the repair with a finely painted network of cracks, to preserve the uniformity of appearance.

On rare occasions, wide cracks may occur in the painting, due to shrinkage, and can be very distracting. In these cases the cracks can be

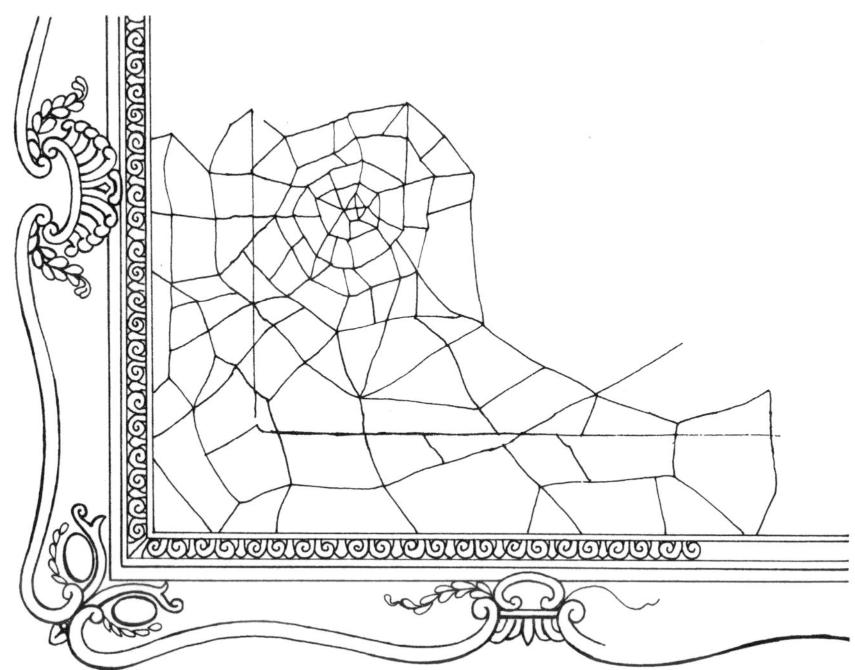

The outline of the stretcher showing through in the pattern of the cracks

repainted in colour to match, but often this only camouflages the defect and in some opinions they are best left, leaving the picture, as the experts say, in an 'honest' condition.

It may come as a surprise to the amateur art enthusiast to realise that very many signed paintings do not in fact bear a signature which was put on by the artist or is even contemporary with the painting. Here craquelure helps establish the authenticity or lack of it of the signature. Obviously if the signature is of the same date as the painting, the cracks will go through the paint of the signature as well as that of the background. When this is not the case, it may reasonably be assumed that the signature has been added later. In art-saleroom parlance, when a painting 'bears signature', it is implied that it bears false signature.

However, armed with this knowledge of craquelure to date a painting, do not be too hasty in labelling the Dutch seventeenth-century painting in the local museum a modern fake because it exhibits no cracks at all. Some paintings on wooden panels or copper show no cracks at all even though they may be three to four hundred years old. On the other hand, occasionally one may see a more recent painting where all the brown pigments show multitudinous, unsightly cracks. This disfiguring feature is due to a bitumen constitutent in brown paint which in fact never dries properly and takes on this unsightly thickening cracking which is hard to describe but can be seen in many of the portrait paintings by the famous painter Sir Joshua Reynolds. It cannot be remedied.

Oil paintings

Flaking paint

Sometimes, unfortunately, the paint on a picture has flaked away. This may be due to various causes, such as defects in the preparation of the canvas or panel, or scratches or accidents happening over the years. The most important aspect of flaking paint is to try to find or keep the pieces of paint which have flaked away. This may sound an improbable task, but in a good many cases of extensive flaking in nineteenth-century paintings, where they have been framed behind glass, the pieces of flaked paint are to be found contained within the space between the canvas and the glass. That this is important can be seen from the prices sometimes realised at auction by paintings in this condition, when the picture has never been taken out of its frame, and all the missing pieces can be seen. A skilled restorer is able to piece all the flaked areas back into place like in a jigsaw puzzle, adhering each piece using a beeswax and hot spatula-tip technique. Beeswax has a fairly low melting point and by placing each piece into its respective position after coating with a thin wax layer, gentle touching with the hot spatula is sufficient to melt the wax. When the heat is removed the wax re-solidifies, leaving the flaked piece held firmly in position, usually providing a perfect repair.

Should you therefore have a valuable oil painting where some flaking has occurred, it would be important to get it and the pieces to a skilled restorer as soon as possible. If the picture is not of that importance, a quick adhesion, using the beeswax technique and a spoon handle instead of a spatula, heated in near boiling water, may suffice. Alternatively you may even be able to glue the pieces back with a good adhesive.

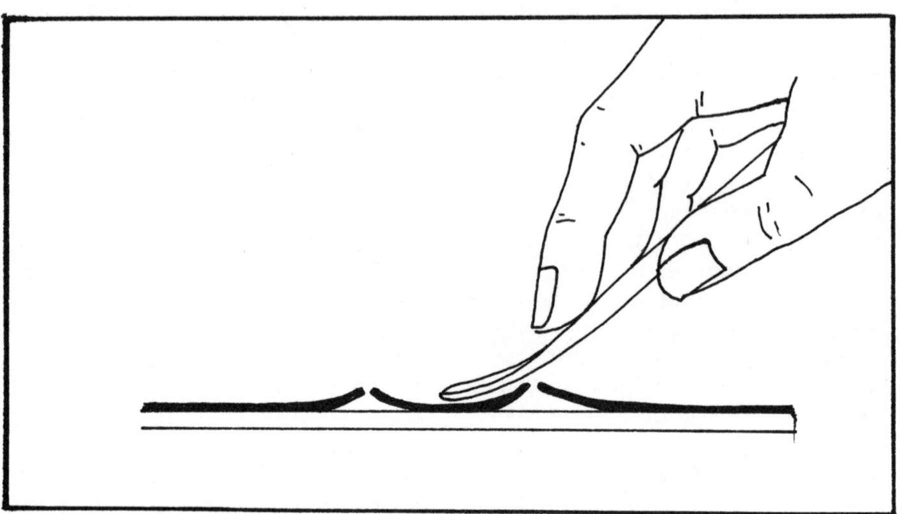

Re-adhering flaking paint using a heated spatula

Often, however, the flaked-off pieces are long gone, and pieces of the white 'ground' (preparation) now show, proving to be very distracting. If a quick improvement in the appearance of the picture is required, it is enough just to repaint these missing areas with either oil paint, acrylic paint or watercolour, using a colour which matches the surroundings. This technique will only stand up to casual observation, for, if viewed from the side, the depression left as a result of the thickness of paint having been lost, will show, and shadow formation and the uneven texture will reveal the damaged area. This is why a skilled painting restorer will not only repaint a flaked area but will use a filling medium on the missing area to ensure that a continuation of surface is made, and only then repaint.

For simplicity, if a repair of this type is to be made by the amateur, ordinary putty, even acrylic paint, or some other filler could be applied, with the aid of a palette knife carefully handled. It also helps if a little paint of the approximate colour of the surroundings is mixed with the filler, because if, after completing the filling and leaving it to dry, a purely white-filled area is left, then several coats of thin paint on top would be needed to cover over the glaring white. If the filler is approximately the right colour then this added complication can be avoided.

If the amateur, following these instructions, just repaints the lost area, or uses a putty filler, no permanent alteration to the picture has been done. If at a later stage a skilled restorer wishes to obtain a perfect finish, both these repair techniques could easily be reversed by him, with no damage to the painting having been done.

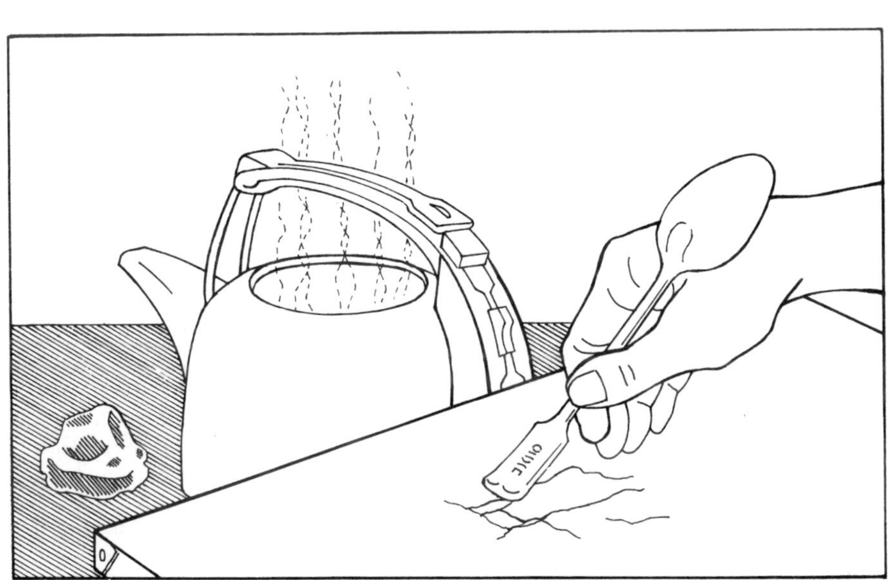

A quick adhesion using beeswax and a hot spoon handle

Oil paintings

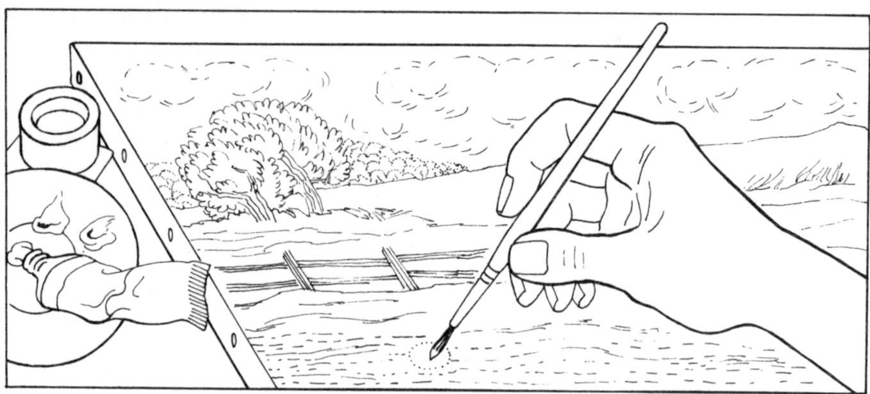

Repainting a missing portion using a stippling technique

Repainting

To enable one to properly ascertain the colours of a painting, it is often necessary first to give the painting a very diluted coat of varnish so that the true colours can be seen.

Some restorers keep to 'in-painting' only, so that if a piece of blue sky is being restored, blue paint will be applied to the missing portion only, using a stippling technique, and not to any surrounding areas. This practice has the advantage of keeping the adulteration of the painting down to the minimum; however it will usually be observable if examined carefully.

On the other hand, restorers who have a good knowledge of what paintings should look like, when restoring for example a small area of sky, may find it necessary to build up a cloud or add another branch to a tree or something similar, so that the final repair will be completely undetectable to the naked eye. The obvious disadvantage is that one does need to have a great deal of skill and also that it does increase the amount of repainted area in the picture.

It might come as a surprise to most people to see some gallery pictures, which superficially appear in perfect condition, illuminated using an ultraviolet picture inspection lamp. Under these conditions, paint which is old takes on a ghostly and translucent appearance, whereas the repainted areas stand out boldly in black. If you have just invested in an expensive painting it is probably not advisable to inspect it through such a lamp as it may cause disappointment! However, it is now widely recognised that many, if not most, good paintings have had certain small restorations completed on them and it becomes of serious concern only when restoration exceeds 25 per cent of the picture surface.

Cleaning surface grime

It must be admitted that the cleaning of an old, yellowed, oil painting is a fascinating experience, as the original colours and quality of painting are gradually revealed. However, holding to the old adage that 'an ounce of prevention is worth a pound of cure', it might be advisable first to state that the best way to ensure no surface

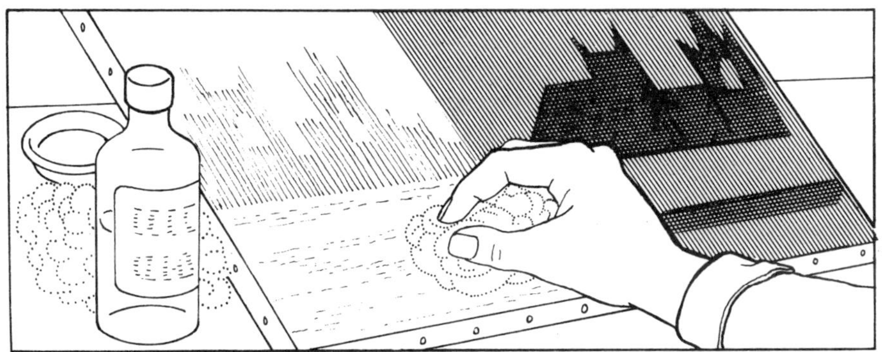

Surface grime should be carefully removed using cotton wool soaked in white spirit

grime builds up is to dust the painting regularly and carefully with a feather duster or something similar. Do not rub with a rag as this might cause a piece of paint to flake away.

If the painting has an old coat of varnish and is covered in dust and grime, a piece of cotton wool soaked in white spirit and carefully wiped over the surface will take off the surface dirt. It will also reveal, to a degree, the brightness of the picture underneath, as it will make the picture appear semi-varnished until it evaporates, whereupon the picture will once more resume its duller appearance. As long as the painting is in oil paint and older than five years, white spirit will not harm it at all. In fact, the older it is, the safer. Only if the painting has been recently varnished would the white spirit be inadvisable, as it would tend to dissolve the new varnish. Old varnish or paint will be completely unaffected.

Sometimes a white bloom will be seen over the surface of the picture. This is quite a common feature and if, when wiped over with white spirit, it is seen to disappear but return when the white spirit has evaporated, it will only be necessary to revarnish the oil painting with a good varnish to ensure the disappearance of this unsightly bloom (see page 14).

On rare occasions, usually with paintings of little value which were probably not varnished on completion, surface grime can become quite ingrained. *If you are sure the painting is of little value,* then to achieve an improvement, wipe the surface gently using cotton wool buds soaked in an ammonia solution (10 per cent Scrubbs cloudy ammonia solution diluted with an equal amount of water) but be careful not to rub hard, and only work on a small area at a time, with the picture lying flat, and after cleaning a small area, dry it using clean swabs.

The danger of this technique is that it will remove paint as well as dirt and so should only be tried on oil paintings of very little value, or by someone with good experience of oil paintings. Hot soapy water is never to be recommended for cleaning old oil paint as it will only partially remove grime and will loosen the paint from the ground of the canvas, leaving a rubbed, semi-clean painting as a result.

After removal of surface grime, the next stage involves removal of the old varnish.

Oil paintings

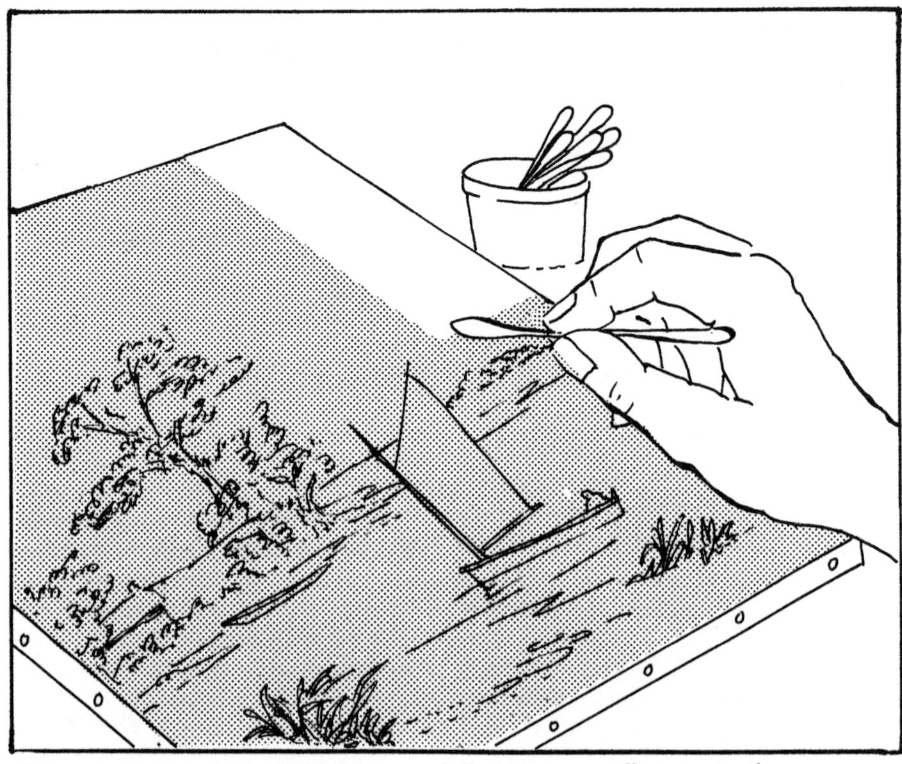

When removing old varnish, work carefully on very small areas at a time

Removing old varnish

If the varnish is very new, white spirit might suffice, especially as modern varnishes should not become progressively more insoluble as the older varnishes have. However, the problem now encountered is that the solvents available for old varnishes may also attack or dissolve the underlying paint. Thus any removal of old varnish must be done in a very careful manner, using cotton wool swabs on a very small area at a time. Typical solvents are acetone, methyl alchohol and ethyl alchohol. These organic solvents can be diluted using white spirit. Acetone is probably one of the most commonly used solvents but it has its disadvantages. Diluted ammonia solution can also be used.

However, it is also interesting to note that most people would start to clean a painting by beginning on the sky; here lies the reason for many a disaster over cleaning a painting. Sky colours – white, greys and blues – are the safest colours to clean with solvents and as he sees a crisp clean sky revealed, the amateur may fall into the trap of thinking that the cleaning is going well and easily. In the hurry to complete it, it is easy to forget caution and, using the same concentration of solvent on the foreground of the picture, disaster occurs because colours such as greens, reds and

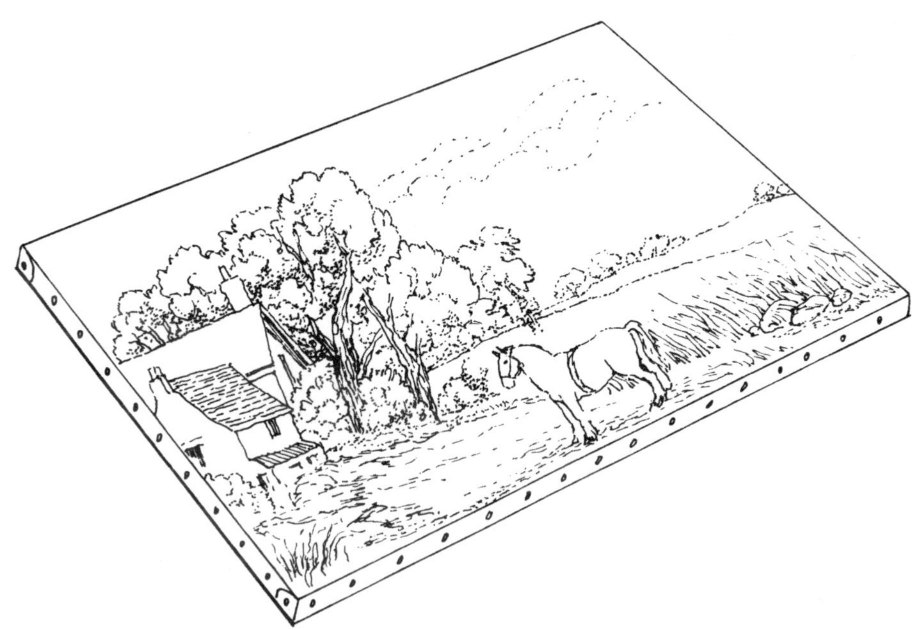

Sky colours are the easiest to clean. Exercise great caution especially when cleaning the foreground of a painting

especially browns are much more easily removed. The danger lies in possible over-cleaning of the detail of these colours which leaves a picture devoid of the detail which the artist originally laboured over. This sad story has occurred many times even with some important paintings in public collections, resulting in the very 'thin' appearance of these 'earth' colours in many of them.

If in doubt on the removal of old varnish in dark detailed areas, be over-cautious, even if necessary leaving the old varnish on and relying on a new coat of varnish to brighten it. It is better to leave it like this than continue and lose the detail of the painting. Most professional restorers recognise that complete varnish removal, even with the greatest of care, does often remove a little paint. They, however, will be more able to replace and strengthen weak areas than will the average person.

Sometimes, after cleaning, a white bloom will be seen on some parts of the painting, leaving the would-be renovator concerned that the painting is ruined.

This blanching is commonly met with and will disappear on revarnishing, but when seen it does show that caution to avoid overcleaning must be taken.

Oil paintings

Revarnishing

The varnishing of a painting is a most important operation as not only does it give the colours of the painting a glowing appearance, but also provides the painting with its future protection. However, a thick glossy coat of varnish, while allowing all the original colours to shine brilliantly and also offering good protection, does look rather glossy and brassy. A more matt finish on the other hand is difficult to apply and as matt varnishes involve the addition of wax as a matting agent, they offer less protection but give a much more pleasing appearance to the eye.

A suitable compromise can be achieved by various means. In preparing the oil painting for varnishing, ensure that the picture is absolutely clean and free from anything like fluff or dirt; it is also advisable to work in a warm room with the picture also warm. Dilute the varnish down to 2 parts varnish, 1 part white spirit, and, using a wide brush with the painting lying flat, apply the varnish with criss-cross strokes, until all the paint has been covered in a varnish film. A second coat may be considered advisable after the first has dried. A certain degree of reduction of gloss may be achieved by continuing to brush even whilst the varnish is tacky and, by using a stippling technique, a certain rendering down can be achieved, at the same time ensuring thorough impregnation with varnish. If a more matt effect is desired, a wax matt varnish can be mixed with the gloss, depending on the degree of mattness required. However, this method will

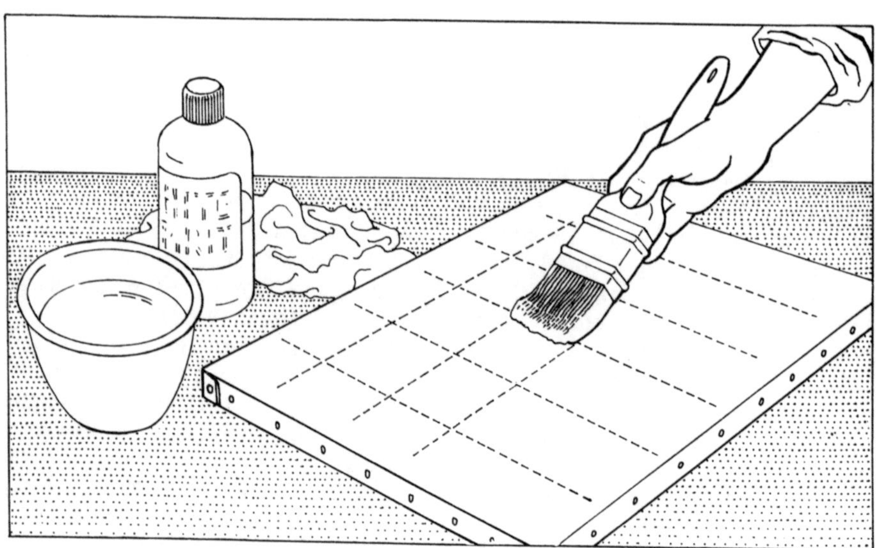

Applying varnish with a brush, using criss-cross strokes

require the varnish and brush being heated slightly to dissolve the matt wax varnish.

Sometimes an attractive finish can be achieved by applying one of the commercial soft wax picture varnishes, after the brushed varnish has dried hard. The wax paste is applied using a soft cloth and gently polished when dry.

Nowadays the use of spraying techniques has introduced new scope into the realm of picture appearance. Small spray units can be purchased or varnish can be purchased in spray cans. The advantage of spraying is that it applies a very even coating of varnish and also, using the spray bottle warmed, matt varnishes can be applied, giving acceptable 'eggshell' finishes. However, unless used carefully, spray units only impart a very thin film of varnish which may offer slightly less protection for the future.

The picture should be sprayed from a distance of 10–15in, with the picture positioned vertically, using a very light side-to-side technique, being careful not to allow varnish to become saturated in any one part of the picture. To prevent the varnish running, varnish lightly three or four times rather than trying to complete the spraying in one operation.

Whichever way of applying the varnish is chosen, remember always to take the greatest care over cleanliness and the removal of fluff and dirt. In this connection, do not wear woollen clothing while brushing, or a few hair fibres will adhere to the picture surface, which will irritate the perfectionist ever after! One famous restorer chose to complete his varnishing in a greenhouse, where the air had been previously damped down by a water spray to remove dust particles.

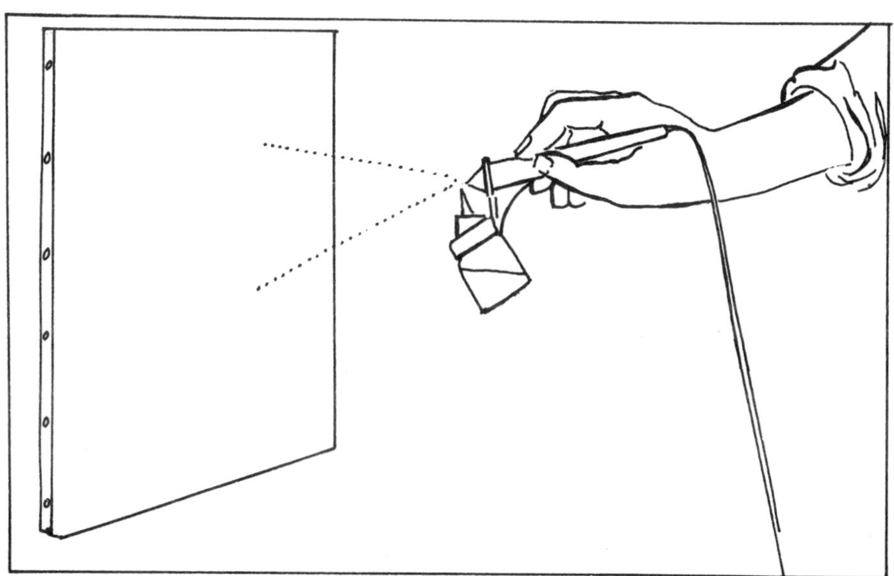

Spray varnishing

Oil paintings

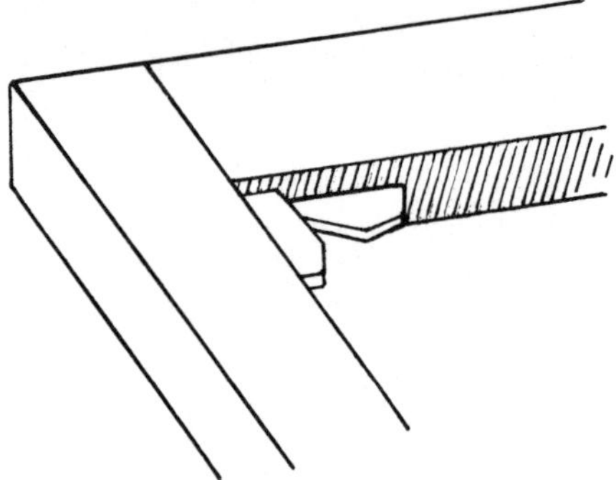

Reverse of a canvas showing wedges

Tightening canvas

Occasionally the canvas of a painting may become slack and the painting sags or shows bumps. The support of the canvas, called the stretcher, enables this condition to be remedied. Canvas is usually attached to the stretcher by means of tacks and it might appear that the only way to treat the condition would be to re-tack all around, but fortunately this is seldom necessary. Viewed from the back it will be seen that each corner of the stretcher is joined by means of tongue and groove, with small pieces of wood known as wedges left inserted. If these wedges are given a careful tap they will open the wooden stretcher very slightly and so tauten the canvas. However, care is necessary here so that the wedges are only tapped gently and in the direction needed, to overcome the sagging. In some very old paintings the wedges may not still be in existence but usually the stretcher will show slots at the corners where pieces of wood may be fitted in as wedges. Some long established bumps may need the assistance of a warm iron applied from the back.

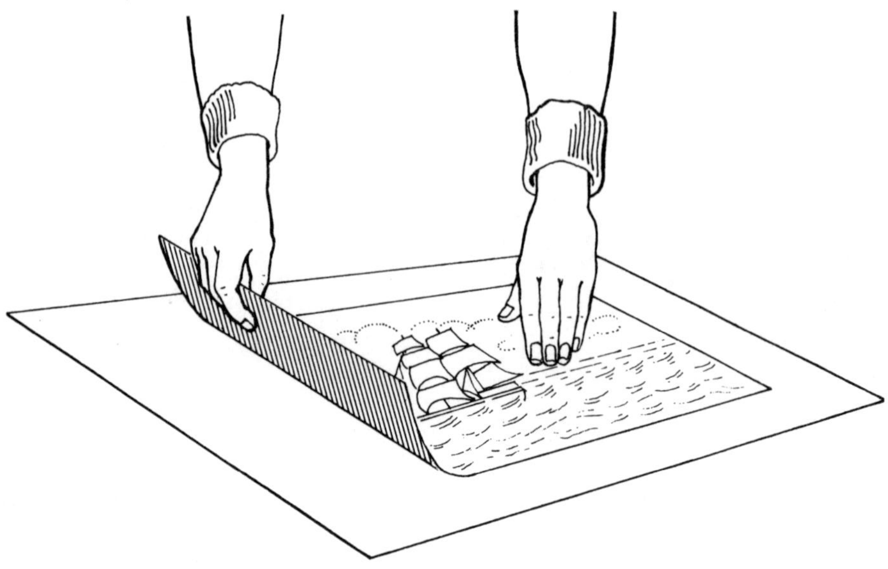

Re-lining a canvas

Repairing canvas

Very many paintings have suffered rips or holes during their existence. An important portrait I once owned had been used previously by a descendant of the subject as a fencing partner and had consequently received minor 'wounds'. Cromwell's troops are reported to have taken delight in shooting at family portraits of Royalist families, a special trick being shooting out the eyes.

Of course most rips, tears and holes have not been made in such spectacular ways and are much more likely to have been caused by leaning the picture against a chair, forgetting about it and an accident ensuing when the dog comes running in!

In the case of extensive rips, re-lining is often called for. Re-lining involves cutting the picture around the edge so that it is freed from its old stretcher. The ripped or holed painting is then adhered on to a new canvas and cleaned as necessary. Finally the new canvas is tacked on to the old stretcher, tightened, restored and revarnished.

Modern restoration techniques have developed what are known as 'vacuum hot-tables' for re-lining canvases, using a hot wax medium as an adhesive and a partial vacuum to press the two canvases together. Obviously this method of re-lining will be beyond the scope of the average renovator and should only be performed by a skilled restorer. Nowadays some restorers prefer canvases to be re-lined using other adhesives, even water soluble pastes, which are more easily removable in the future. To re-line a non-important painting, a flour paste and some thymol crystals (acting as a fungicide) would suffice to perform a fairly simple re-lining operation well within the abilities of a reasonably careful operator.

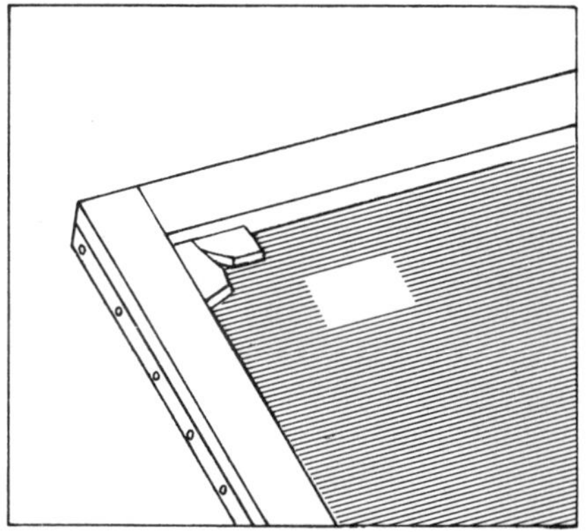

Repairing a small tear from the back of the canvas

A small rip where the edges meet can be repaired in the following way. Working from the back, apply a contact glue to the torn edges. Lay the painting flat, position the torn edges together, apply a piece of brown paper over the repair and, using a weighted book as a press, leave until dry. After the glue has hardened, peel off the paper. This method has the advantage of being almost invisible from behind and one does not have to use a patch, which, with the passage of time, may make its shape visible on the front surface of the painting.

After joining a rip it will usually be necessary to fill in carefully any missing areas, thus providing a uniform texture to the surface of the painting, making it ready for any repainting that is necessary. Sometimes it is helpful to impart a slight weave texture to any filling, to emulate surface texture of the canvas. This effect can be achieved by gently pressing a piece of similar canvas on to the filler while it is still soft.

Oil paintings

Paintings on wood

Many paintings have been painted on materials other than canvas; wood prepared for painting on has been known from the earliest times. The important fourteenth and fifteenth-century paintings are mainly executed on well prepared wooden boards. The correct way to refer to paintings on wood is 'on panel.' Sometimes the paint is directly applied on to the wood, revealing the texture of the grain in the completed picture, but usually panels are prepared by being rubbed down well and then covered with a smooth preparation or 'ground' made from plaster of Paris (gesso).

The main renovation necessary results from the rather distressing and distracting fact that panels are prone to crack apart. This was brought to public attention rather spectacularly some years ago, when Rubens's famous masterpiece 'The Chateau de Steen', in the National Gallery, suddenly developed an horrific split, accompanied by a loud crack. The only available course is simply to glue the panel back together with a good wood glue. It is important that this be done as soon as possible so that the internal stresses and strains of the wood do not further warp the panel and allow it to become accommodated permanently to its new cracked appearance. The re-glueing can be done using standard woodworkers' tools and clamps, being careful not to leave any glue on the surface. Occasionally, to combat warping and to hold a panel together, a supporting framework known as a 'cradle' is built on to the back of the panel; this operation is best left to a professional.

Treatment for woodworm can be undertaken from the back of the panel and any surface holes filled and re-painted.

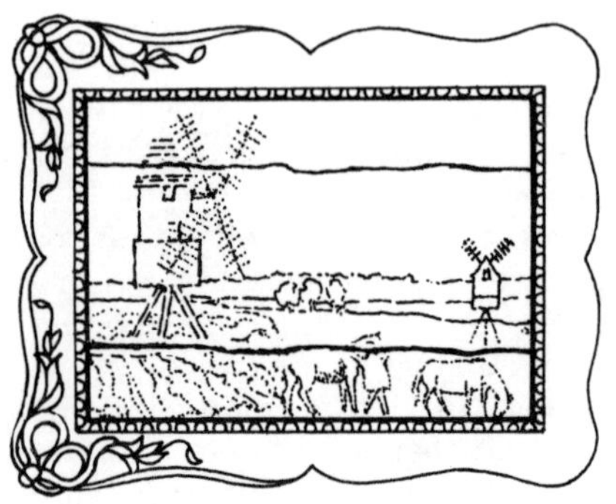

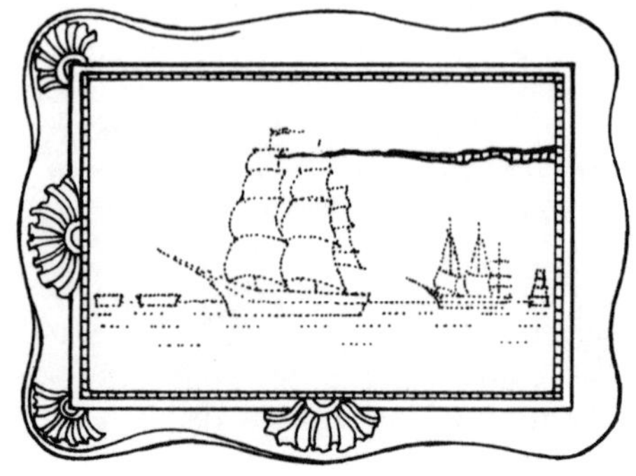

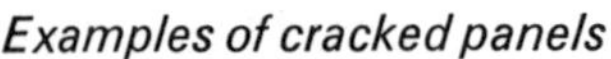

Examples of cracked panels

Paintings on board

As a convenient, lighter means of providing a paintable surface, millboard, or sometimes even cardboard, has been used. The problem of cracking is rarely met with but sometimes a bump or lump may be in evidence, due to some accident or other misfortune. This is a rather difficult problem to deal with because, by virtue of its stiffness, millboard or cardboard will not usually allow itself to be easily pressed back flat. The only way to alleviate the unsightly lump or depression is to very carefully cut or scrape away at the back of the board beneath the bump, until one is nearly at the paint layer – at which point great care must be taken. It will now be found possible to either flatten the bump or push out the dent. Lay the painting flat, fill the hollowed-out area with a hard-setting glue, then lay a piece of paper over the glue to seal it in. Place a book over the top and leave to set hard. This will alleviate what would otherwise be an unrestorable defect.

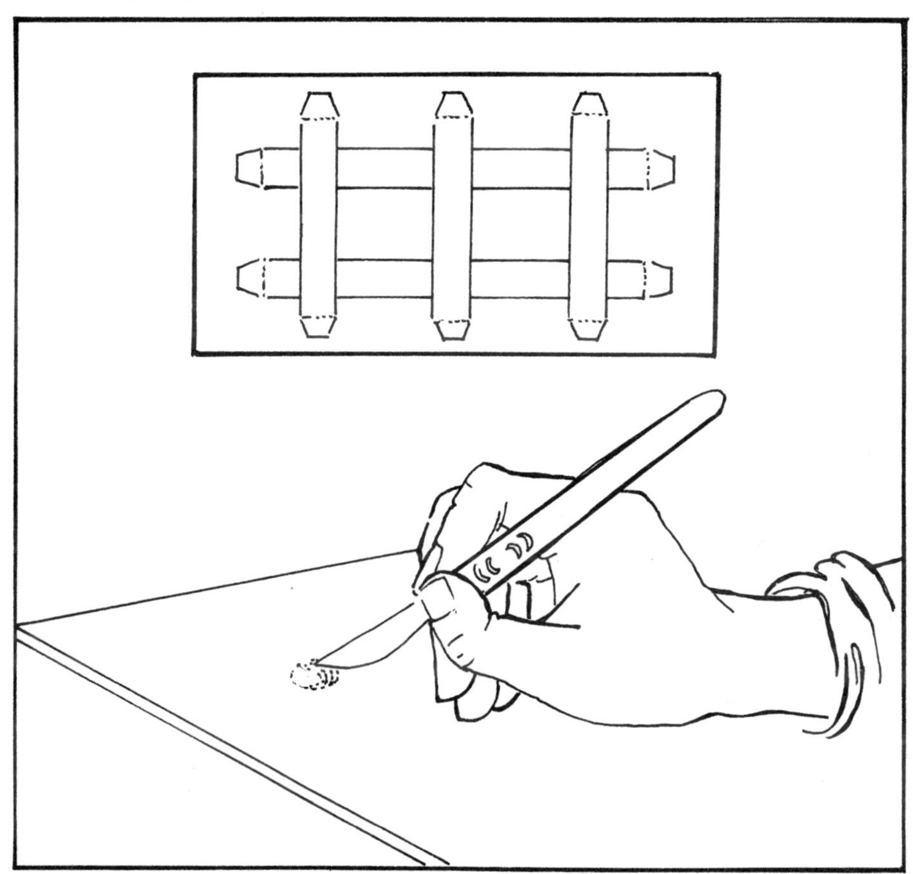

(above) *A supporting 'cradle' on the back of a painting;* (below) *Scraping away the back of a bump*

Watercolours

A definition

Painting in watercolours has been known for many centuries and developed long before the use of oil paint. Interestingly it has been especially an English pursuit for the past two centuries, competence in its use being considered at one time an essential part of education. Consequently, as a legacy of the Victorian era, there are many skilful paintings executed in this medium.

Some of the terms may need explanation. 'Watercolour wash' is the term used to describe watercolour diluted with water only, painted across a sheet of paper. 'Pen, ink and watercolour' implies a pen and ink outline, with watercoloured areas. 'Guache' is the term given to watercolour mixed with the thick pigment, Chinese white, which gives guache an almost oil-paint opaqueness rather than the transparent delicate effect of a watercolour wash. Guache may also be referred to as 'bodycolour' or 'watercolour heightened with white'.

The most common defect occurring with watercolours is that of 'foxing' (brown-spot staining).

Foxing

The unsightly brown spots seen on watercolours and pages of old books have long been the subject of debate as to cause and origin. However, you can understand foxing only too well if you observe what happens to uncovered jam, soup or even an old pair of leather shoes left in a warm damp place. They all develop spots of mould and this is what foxing actually is, occurring on and in the paper. Many a person having a foxed watercolour has taken it out of its frame and been dismayed to see that the brown spots are not just on the glass of the picture but are actually in the paper, sometimes in evidence on both front and back of the paper or card used for the painting. Usually the discoloration is brown but it may also occur as black spotting.

An important point to realise is that by correct chemical treatment the discoloration can be completely removed and the mould killed, leaving the watercolour quite unblemished. If the brown spots have been either scratched out, painted over, locally bleached white or in any other way tampered with, then the watercolour will have been to a greater or lesser degree permanently damaged. Any repainting necessary with water-

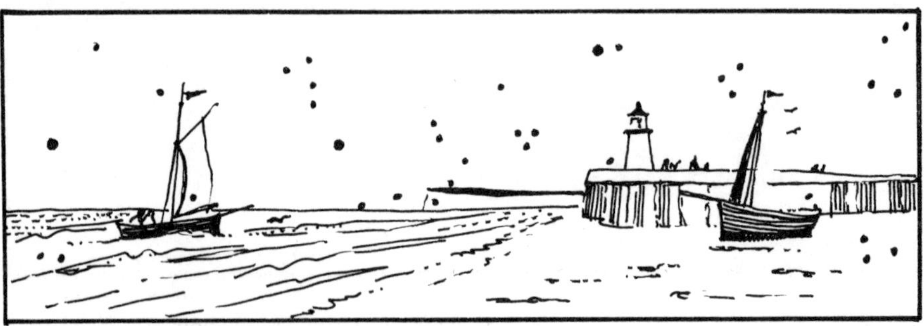

How foxing often appears

colours is a much more difficult operation to complete successfully and cannot easily be reversed or tried again.

The correct way to treat foxing in watercolours so that no retouching is ever necessary is basically that of treating with a bleaching or oxidising agent, usually whilst the watercolour is wet. Due to the obvious difficulty of handling and other variable factors, *valuable watercolours should always be left to an expert*. So if you know of no one reliable, it is better to leave it foxed and enjoy its appearance of antiquity rather than have to live with a bleached, washed-out, ruined watercolour which will also have a drastically reduced value.

How to stop foxing getting worse

As we have already seen, foxing is due to a mould growth, thus any steps to stop mould formation will be of benefit. The present museum practice is to use a fungicide-impregnated paper either inserted behind the watercolour in the frame or, if the watercolour is kept in a portfolio or drawer, a sheet is kept in with the portfolio.

The preparation of your own fungicide-impregnated paper is, in fact, quite elementary. Obtain a small amount of thymol crystals from the local chemist. Dissolve several crystals in a small amount of warm water, and when they are dissolved, allow this solution to drip on to a clean sheet of white blotting paper. After it has dried, you will have a thymol-impregnated sheet of paper, which has fungicidal properties. It may be necessary to repeat the operation after several years so that the fungicidal properties are renewed.

Interestingly it is now the practice of some museums to leave old drawings and watercolours in their foxed state, just ensuring that the mould growth does not get any worse by storing them in portfolios with the thymol-impregnated paper present. This is because, during the bleaching process involved in removing foxing, there may, as a side effect, be a slight deterioration in the cellulose formation of the paper – perhaps shortening its life – no matter how carefully controlled the process is or how well the drawing looks afterwards. However, as well made paper does seem to have an amazingly long life, it is a case of weighing up the short- and long-term aims.

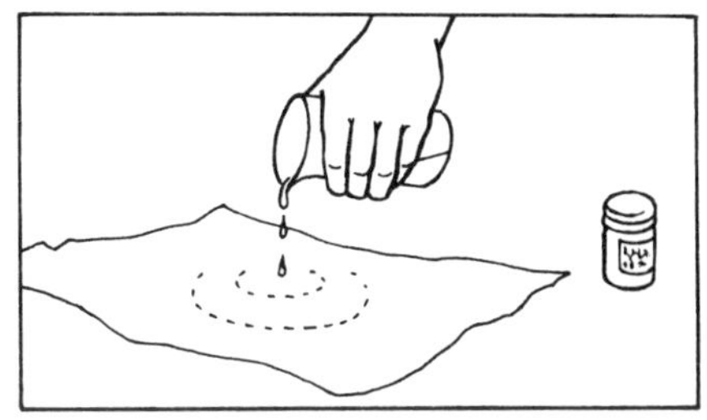

Preparing a fungicide-impregnated paper

No valuable or well loved watercolour or drawing should be kept in a damp place or left to hang on a damp wall, as this will of course provide all the conditions for mould. On the other hand do not remove the watercolour to a position where sunlight may strike it, as this will cause fading and possible acidification (browning) of the paper. As modern technology and scholarship increases with respect to foxing, it is not as serious as it might appear to be. So, if in evidence on any of your watercolours, drawings or prints, you should not worry too much.

Watercolours

Damp staining

Damp stains, or water stains as they are sometimes referred to, often occur as a result of a burst water-pipe or a flood or some other partial soaking. After drying, the watercolour or print is seen to bear a stain at the edges of the soaked area. Professional wet-cleaning techniques can usually completely remove such staining, by the same process used to remove foxing. However you can avoid the formation of a water stain if you know how to deal with the watercolour at the time of the accident. For example if you were unfortunate enough to spill a cup of tea or water over an unframed watercolour, the natural tendency might be to dry off the soaked parts of the watercolour with clean blotting paper. As a result of taking this action you would be left with a stain on the picture. Rather you should take what at first might appear to be the most drastic action – that of running a bath of cold water and immediately immersing *all* the watercolour; after leaving it immersed for, say, fifteen minutes, remove it from the bath and allow to dry gently. Although this may sound highly dangerous for a watercolour painting, you will be surprised to note that no running or loss of watercolour will be observed, and as all the watercolour has been immersed and suffused with water, any stain or chemical in the solution will have been diluted and washed away and no blemish will be left. Most watercolours can stand immersion in cold water for several hours; many that are thinly painted in watercolour wash would be unaffected by immersion for a week or more. The points to remember are (i) immerse *all* – not just part – of the watercolour in cold water (ii); do it immediately, before the stain dries in.

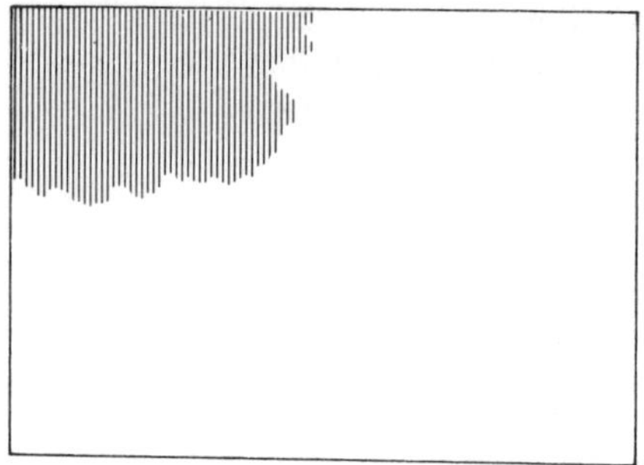

Appearance of damp staining

Cleaning surface grime

Surface grime presents a different problem, and what might appear to be only a slight defect is one of the most difficult to remedy.

If the grime, which sometimes occurs on drawings or watercolours kept unframed, is of long standing, then it may well be that it has become fixed into the paper and is impossible to remove chemically. However, if the watercolour or drawing has any value, you will be well advised not to try this yourself.

You can use a wad of cotton wool soaked in a carbon tetrachloride solution (the dry-cleaning agent), or pure acetone or benzine in the event of any grease-based dirt. Care is needed here however to ensure that the cotton wool is changed as it gets dirty, and also that you wipe over *all* the picture, using a very light technique.

When the grime has occurred only recently then a very soft rubber, used in sweeping strokes, *not a round*

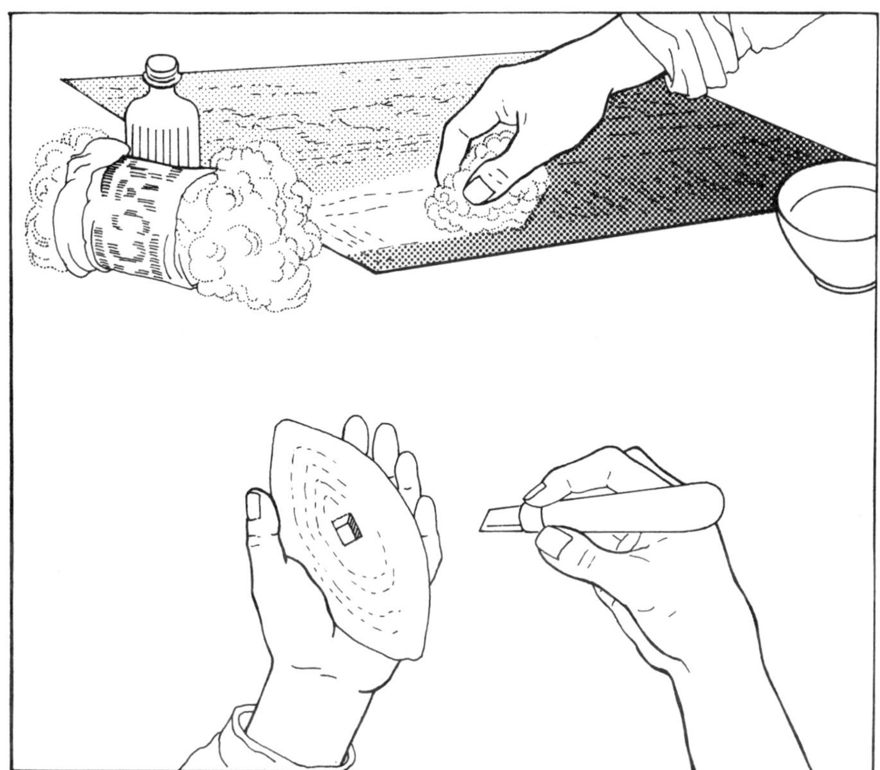

(above) *Take great care when removing surface grime;* (below) *Cutting a piece of cuttlefish bone to use as an abrasive agent*

rubbing technique, should remove the grime. It is important to remove it as soon as possible because if left on for a few years, grime soon becomes fixed into the paper and resists any easy attempt to remove it.

On the rare occasions when ingrained dirt is to be removed and the only way to do so is to abrase it away, it should be remembered that any abrasive action will also remove the paint surface. Thus only on white areas, such as a white cloud or white paper areas, should abrasions be employed. The most effective abrasion agent is in fact white cuttlefish bone as sold for birdcage use. Cut a small cube from the complete shell and, using it skilfully, you can eventually even shave newsprint from the surface of newspaper without rubbing through the paper itself. However, the use of cuttlefish bone as an abrasive is only a last-ditch method of cleaning and if used on a coloured part of a watercolour painting will of course spoil the appearance.

Thus, again in the case of surface grime, prevention is worth a pound of cure and if it is of long standing, one may just have to live with it. These techniques can also be used for cleaning prints.

Watercolours

Mending rips, tears and scratches

The worst type of rip to repair is a scissor-type cut, as you cannot take advantage of the fibrous shredding effect you get with rag-made papers. In a normal rip or tear, if you examine the torn areas carefully, it will be seen that many small fibres are in evidence at the torn edge, and if the rip is put back in the same way it was torn, these fibres can to a certain extent be re-knitted, and instead of a cross-section as in (a) you have in fact the situation as in (b). Thus in the repair (i) must be glued on to (ii) ; if glued the wrong way, then (c) will be the result and an unsightly join will be left. It is possible, using great skill and possibly a tool such as a metal spoon, to press the ripped areas back together so well that an almost invisible repair is made. Usually after glueing the torn edges, a piece of tissue is glued over the back to further strengthen the repair. A thick clear wallpaper glue would be the best adhesive for this type of repair and of course, whilst drying, keep the repair under flat pressure.

In the event of scratches and also sometimes with the edges of a tear, it is necessary to repaint the lost area. Here extreme care is necessary in order to retouch the missing area only and not, in carelessness, to repaint over on to the other, undamaged parts. It is perhaps worth stating that if the scratch is in a blue or very light area of the picture, successfully repainting the area will be very difficult for the amateur, and even for the professional, for that matter ; but if in a dark area, with skill one can make the repair completely invisible. However, if in doubt, consult an expert in the field.

These techniques can also be used for mending prints.

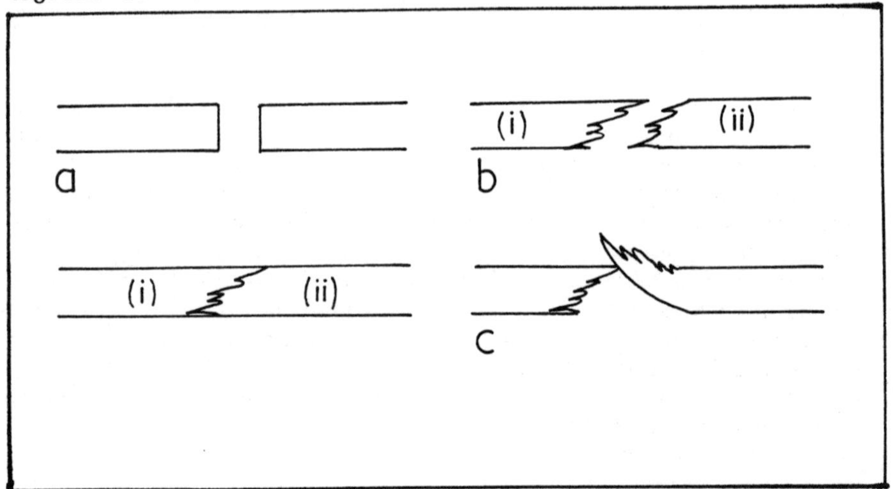

(a) Cross-section of a cut and (b) of a tear; this is easier to repair invisibly if (i) is glued to (ii) and not as in (c)

Straightening buckled watercolours

Watercolour drawing paper, being made from rags, will of course exhibit some of the same qualities as cloth. Consequently the paper will stretch when wet or damp and shrink when dry. Sometimes, after being kept in a damp position, a watercolour is seen to be buckled. If the buckling is not too serious, all that may be necessary to remedy the situation will be to press the watercolour out between two sheets of clean blotting paper and keep it pressed flat for several days. If the buckling is severe it may be necessary to re-stretch the watercolour paper. This principle will be familiar to anyone used to painting in watercolours. The paper is wetted and, in the case of a watercolour, a quick immersion in cold water should suffice. If not wishing to completely immerse the watercolour it is just possible to wet the back of the watercolour with a wad of damp cotton wool. After the paper has partly dried, the edges are taped, using brown-paper gummed tape, to a firm board. When the paper dries, after several days, cut the edges with a sharp knife, and the watercolour should remain in a flat state with all the cockles pulled tight. However, if you own a valuable watercolour or drawing, you would be well advised to leave the re-flattening to an expert as there are many variable factors to consider, such as the condition of the paper. Again, as a very slight proportion of the edges of the work has to be taped over, this may not be advisable with an important watercolour where every area is of value, and some other technique might have to be resorted to.

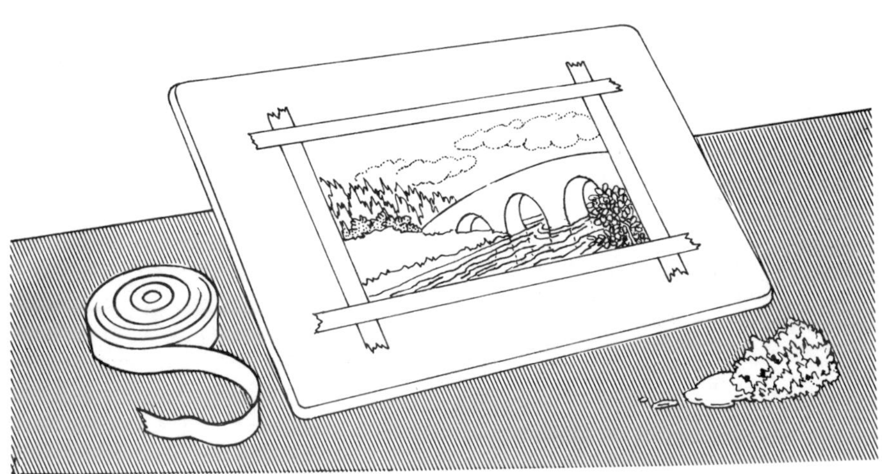

Method of straightening a buckled watercolour

Watercolours

Removing backboard stains

It was an unfortunate practice in the last century to back a frame with thin wooden boards. This seemingly innocent practice has resulted in what are termed 'backboard stains' or 'backboard burns'. Where the boards were joined brown staining appears in the strips down or across the picture, including the mount. If there are knot holes in the boards, these are often reproduced in the picture, the staining having traversed through cardboard $\frac{1}{8}$in thick.

Successful cleaning of backboard staining will usually be beyond the scope of the average renovator as it involves removing the watercolour from the cardboard to which it is often glued. Further, the staining can attack the fibrous make-up of the paper, and the chemical action necessary to remove the stain makes the whole operation a very delicate manoeuvre, and can leave one with a watercolour in two pieces on one's hands. Although I have managed to clean many hundreds of badly back-board-stained watercolours successfully, prevention is obviously important. If you have any valuable watercolours or drawings in old frames which have old boards, it will certainly be in your interest to invest in a new backing board. Nowadays any reputable framer should stock museum-board backing card which has been designed to help preserve watercolours and drawings. A good plywood or hardboard should complete the framing in order to preserve the work of art for future generations.

Backboard staining: if wooden backboards have been joined vertically, the stains appear as illustrated (right)

If backboards have been joined horizontally, the stains appear as illustrated (right)

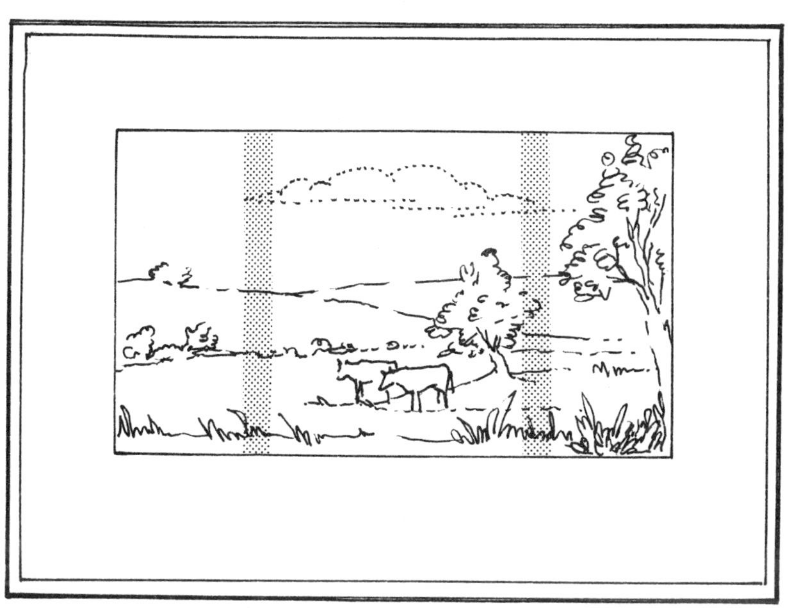

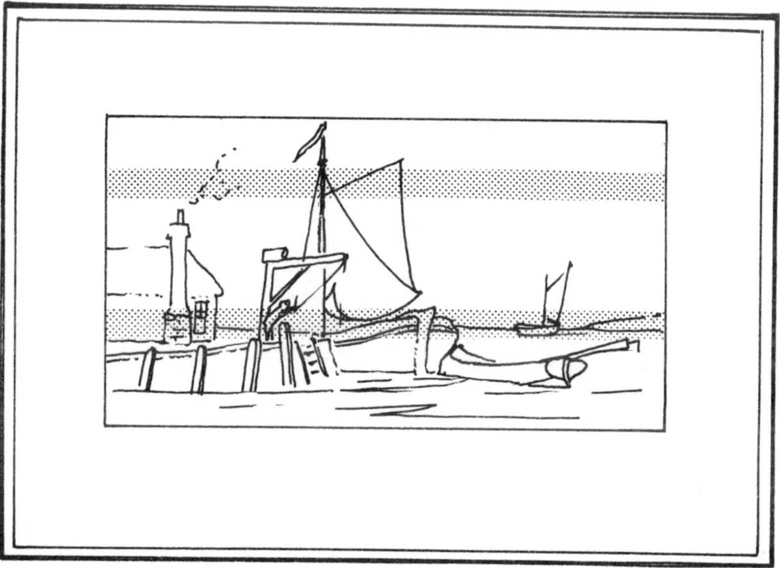

Prints

In almost every home, prints of some description are to be seen hanging on the walls, especially nowadays with the introduction of the limited edition. Possibly each type deserves a special mention.

Modern limited editions

These are usually printed on a modern gloss paper and present no problems in their inherent structure; they will last for an indefinite length of time if framed and preserved correctly. Often the problems come from an exterior source; for example, I once had to clean a modern print which had had a child's boiled sweet stuck to it! If the print has been rolled for a long time or has some bad creases, take it to a reputable framer who will be able to glue it down or otherwise successfully frame it.

If you are framing a limited edition print yourself it is important that you do not, under any circumstances, cut the white border to the print, known as the margin. Often the margin bears a title, signature, or pencilled numbers. If the print does bear numbers, such as '11/50', this means that the print is number eleven of an edition limited to fifty copies. When framed, these details should all be visible as they are part of the print which entitles it to be called a work of art.

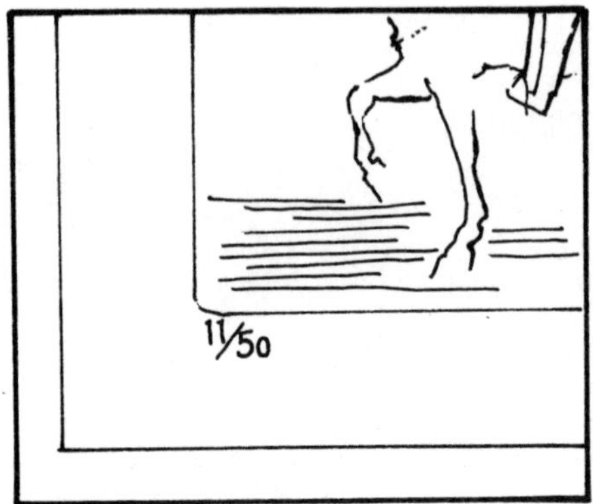

A limited edition print

Old prints

These will be etchings, engravings, mezzotints, woodblocks, aquatints or lithographs. They will usually be printed on a handmade rag-based paper and many of the aspects of renovation as applicable to water-colours and drawings are equally relevant to this type of print. In the case of all these types of print, the margins are most important. In the case of etchings, engravings, mezzo-tints and aquatints, that part of the margin which shows the plate mark should always be displayed within the edges of the mount or frame. This plate mark shows itself as a rec-tangular indentation in the paper surrounding the illustrated subject and is the mark left by the metal plate as the paper was pressed against it to take off the inked details during the print-making process.

Coloured prints of the nineteenth century and beyond are usually of an etched, engraved, aquatinted or litho-graphed base, skilfully hand coloured, and all the points relevant to their renovation are to be found in the section on watercolours, and are really the prerogative of the expert. However, in the case of small black and white engravings and etchings, the following renovations may be successfully resorted to by the amateur.

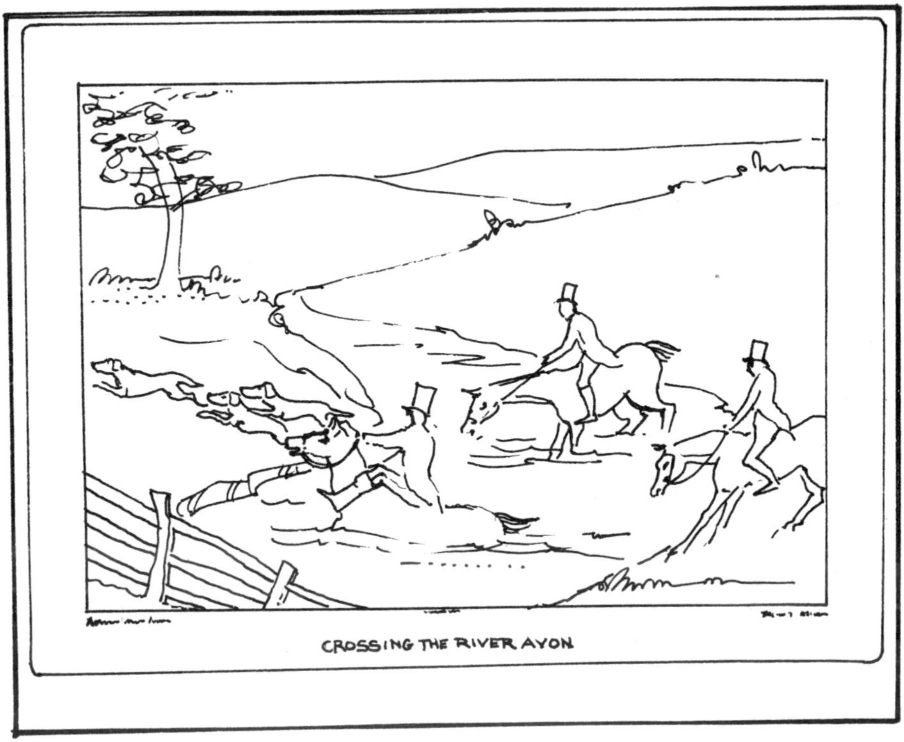

CROSSING THE RIVER AVON

An example of an old hunting print

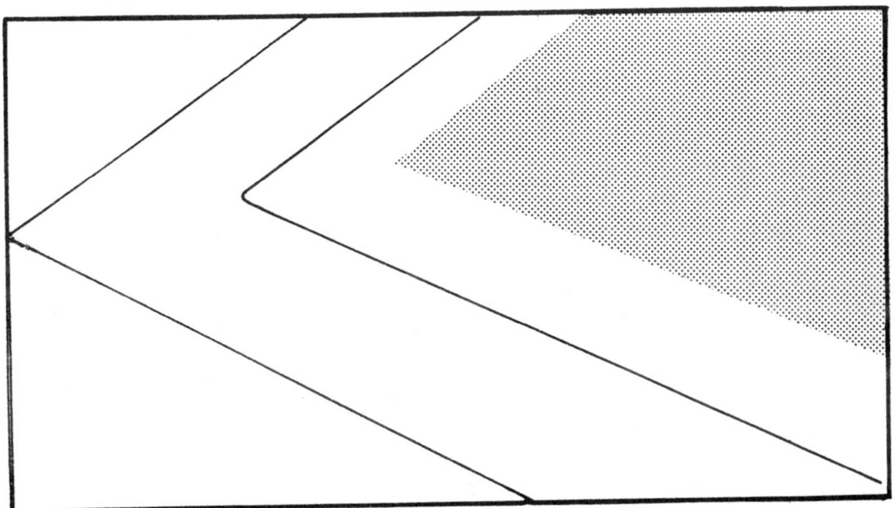

The indented plate mark within the margins of a print should always be displayed

Prints

How to remove foxing from small engravings and etchings

This procedure is an easy renovation for anyone who is reasonably careful; if in doubt try it out on an unimportant print or piece of paper first. The difficulty comes when larger prints have to be handled because of the weakness of the paper when wet. So at home, only use this technique on small or unimportant prints and definitely not on any finely coloured print. Small etchings or engravings can often be found in old travel books, and were originally used as illustrations. If cleaned and coloured they can make an attractive and inexpensive decoration.

To clean the foxing, obtain a tray or dish of a suitable size in which to immerse the print. Make a bleaching solution from one part 1 per cent standardised sodium hypochlorite solution (obtainable from any chemist as the babies' utensil sterilizing agent 'Milton'), mixed with three parts cold water. Pour this bleaching solution into the tray. Run an amount of cold water into a bath or sink to act as a rinsing bath. First immerse the print in the cold-water bath, then, handling with care as now the paper is wet and thus weaker, place it in the bleaching solution and leave for approximately 5 to 10 minutes, after which time the discoloration should start to disappear. The marks in the paper where the foxing was present will still show but should take on a more translucent appearance. After this length of time, remove the print from the bleaching solution and leave it in the water bath for a further 10 minutes in order to dispel the bleaching agent, then remove it and allow it to dry gently. Before the print is completely dry, press it out between two clean, dry sheets of blotting paper. As it dries, so the foxing will be seen to have disappeared. If any foxing does remain after this treatment, repeat the whole operation until the print is clear. The bleaching will also whiten the white-paper margins, and thus brighten the black ink and give an impression of freshness.

This technique will be equally safe with pencil drawings and will even brighten the original pencil strokes.

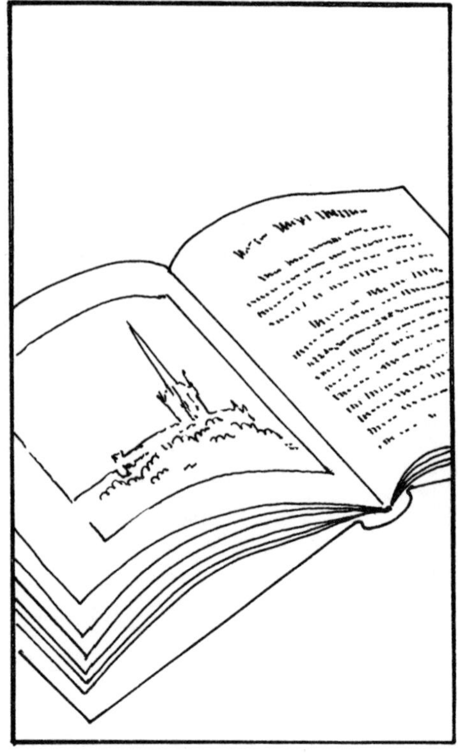

Small etchings or engravings are often found in old travel books

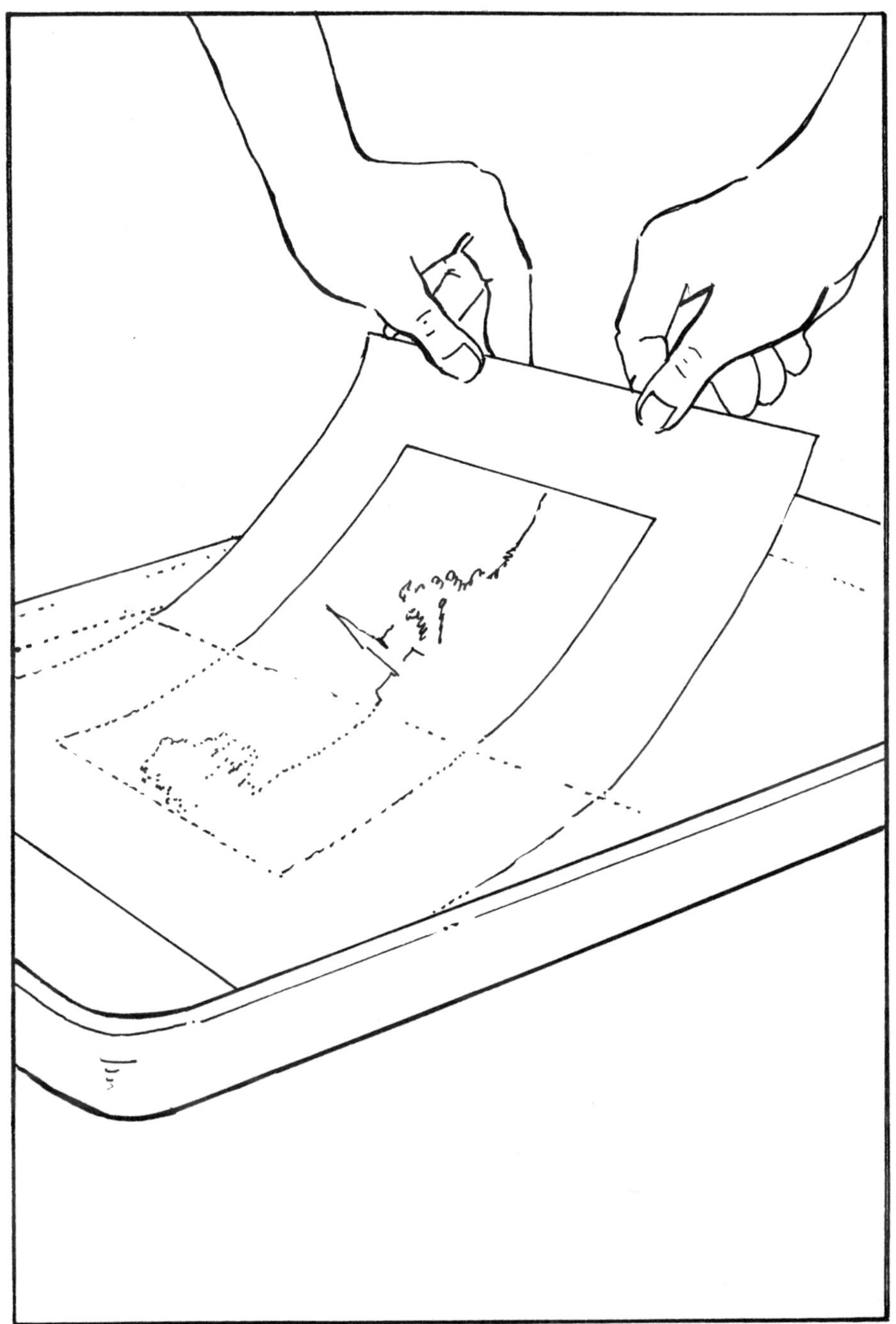

To remove foxing, a print should be immersed first in a cold-water bath, then in bleaching solution, then finally in the water bath again

Prints

Colouring

The colouring of old prints to make them more attractive has always been popular. Many of the old established print publishers of the nineteenth century employed teams of girls or unemployed artists to wash in the various colours, which was sometimes done with exceeding skill. As all the shadows and tones of the picture in most old prints have been included in the final inked version, successful colouring is made much simpler and is purely a technique of applying colour washes to the appropriate areas. Before colouring one's own prints, it might be profitable to look at old coloured prints in the local library, museum or shops and then observe the way the effects are achieved. The most important aspect to remember is at all times to use only a very diluted wash of any colour, then you will avoid garish results.

Use a sable watercolour brush and watercolour paint, and learn to apply an even wash in quick, deft strokes. Often a palette of just six colours is quite sufficient. A typical palette might consist of Naples yellow for light clouds, orange for dark clouds, Prussian blue for sky, rocks or the distance, sap green for trees, yellow ochre for trees and detail and vermilion for red detail. Always remember to work in extremely dilute colour, especially when using Prussian blue. Some colourists prefer to size the prints first, to make the paper less absorbent, facilitating more controllable colouring.

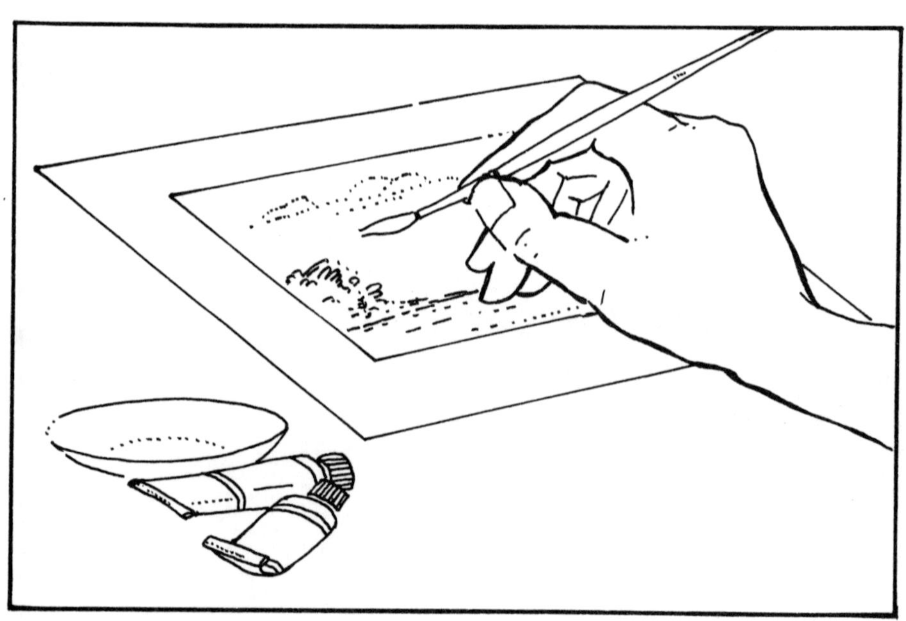

Applying a watercolour wash

Mending rips, tears and holes

Prints can be mended in the same way as watercolours (see page 24); the techniques for cleaning prints are also similar to those for watercolours (see page 22)

It is often useful to keep pieces of old worthless prints so that, if necessary, a piece of etching or engraving of the same type is available if it is found necessary to repair a hole or jagged tear. In the event of a hole it is obviously best to do the repair with a piece of a print of the same texture and thickness. The hole is prepared by chamfering the edges using cuttlefish bone so that the cross-section is as in (a). A piece is then cut out from a similarly etched section of print, slightly larger than the hole to be mended, and chamfered as in (b), then glued into position with a patch of tissue as a backing. Any white areas then remaining can be re-touched after the whole repair has dried, as in (c).

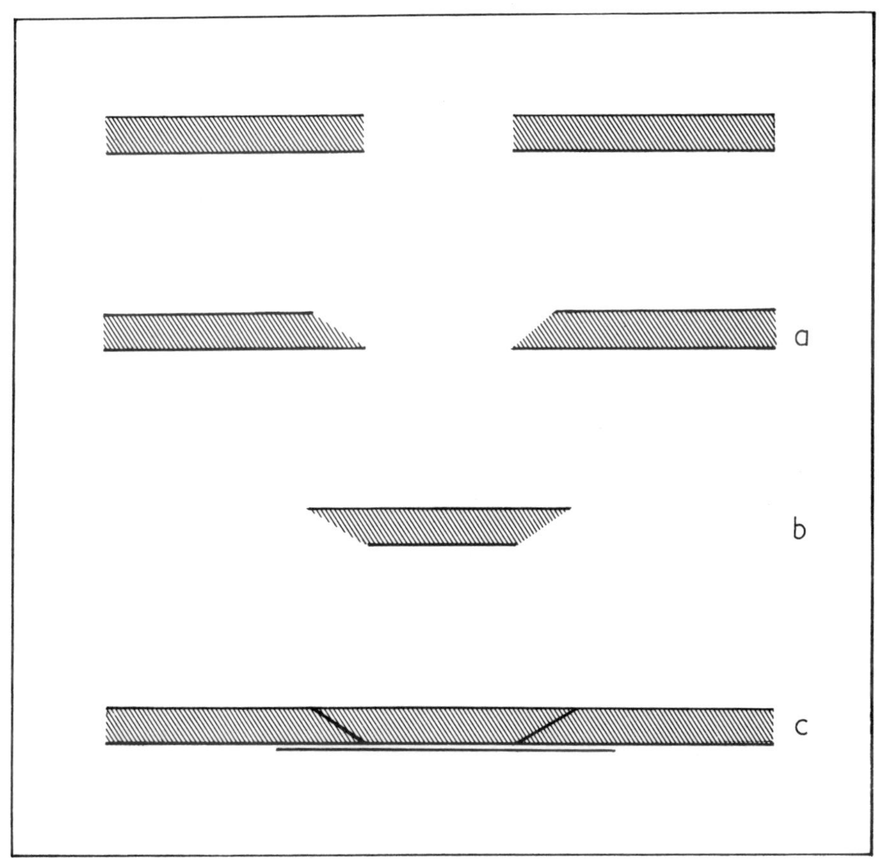

Method of repairing a hole in a print

Other types of picture

Miniatures

The art of miniature painting in England has produced innumerable exquisite works of beauty and great craftsmanship. Often painted on vellum or thin ivory and preserved under glass in narrow frames, they still retain their freshness and charm.

If you have a collection of miniatures, it is wise to find a dry, well aired spot of wall, away from direct sunlight, on which to display them. If stored in drawers or cabinets it is advisable to include in the drawer a sheet of fungicide paper as described previously (see page 21). Occasionally, when a mould may have developed on the glass, it is necessary to take them out of their frames, clean the glass, and when satisfied that the miniature is bone dry, lightly blow and dust it to remove any surface mould. On no account should water-colour miniatures ever be rubbed or wiped with a wet swab, or paint will be instantly removed. As evidenced by the many thousands of miniatures in perfect condition, they would appear to survive the rigours of time exceedingly well, and fortunately the need for restoration is very rare.

Pastels

Unfortunately many pastels have proved themselves to be fertile sites for mould growth. I well remember purchasing an important pastel at one of the London auctions some years ago. It was purchased unseen, surprisingly cheaply. On collection, it was found to be two-thirds covered in mould. However, with time, most pastels become more fixed into the paper and less susceptible to being blown from the surface, and in this case, on removing the pastel from the frame and taking it out from behind the glass, it was found that, with care, using a soft squirrel brush, a good deal of the surface growth could be brushed away without disturbing too much of the original pastel. After slight re-touching this same pastel was re-sold in London at more than twenty times the price of three months previously!

Of course it goes without saying that if you have a pastel, you should use all the means described earlier for inhibiting mould growth so that the need for future restoration can be avoided.

Chinese rice-paper paintings

Produced in Canton and surrounding areas from 1800 to 1880, these abound in salerooms and antique shops around the country. Often of almost incredible fineness, these represent a fairly cheap investment in the fine-art world. Due to being painted on fragile rice paper, they almost invariably develop splits and losses if kept out of the protection of a frame for any length of time. All that can be done then is to glue them down on to a stiff card, positioning them so that the splits are fixed together. On rare occasions with important works, you can insert missing areas using spare rice paper and a filler to fit, but it is not a job recommended if you want to keep an even temper!

Examples of miniatures (above) *and rice-paper paintings*

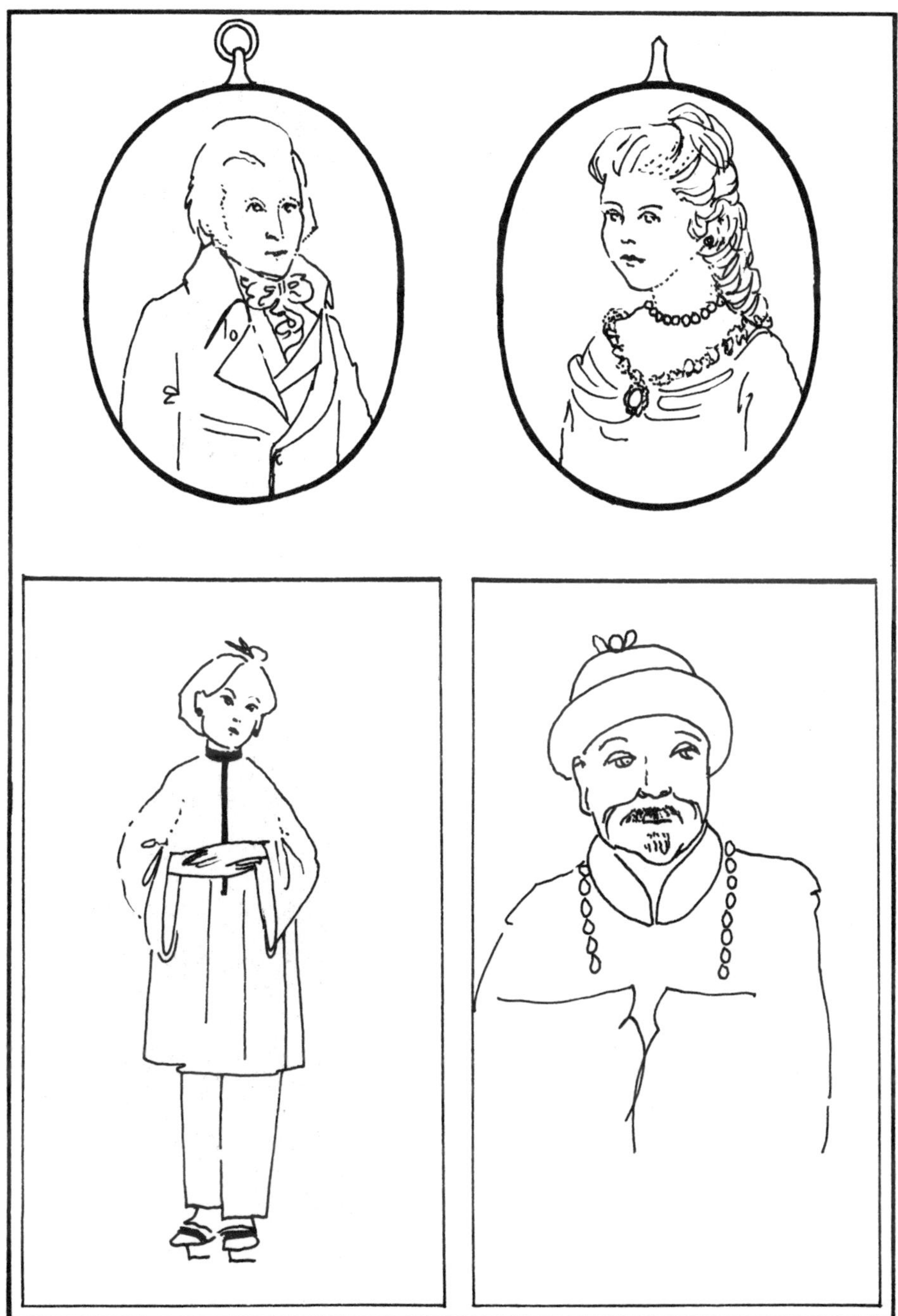

Other types of picture

Silhouettes

Silhouettes, popular in the nineteenth century, have found a revival of interest. They are usually found in good condition. In rare cases it may be necessary to bleach the surrounding card white, as described previously (see page 30). Often with this cleaning process, the black paper silhouette will need re-adhering, so if you do undertake this job yourself, be prepared to see the black paper silhouette floating freely in the bleaching bath.

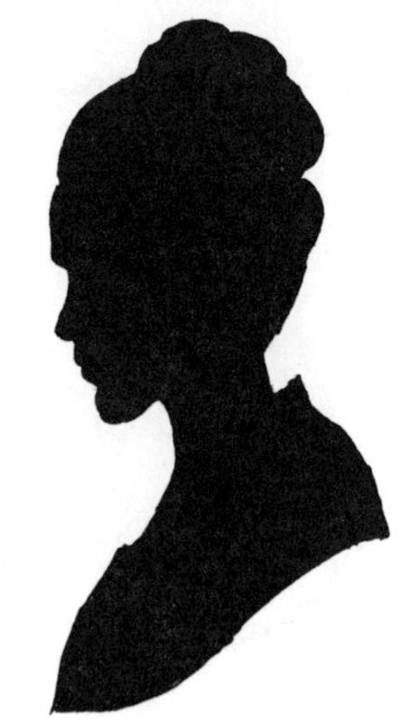

Paintings on glass or porcelain

Usually, apart from being very fragile, paintings on glass or porcelain exhibit no special problems, and may be cleaned by any of the methods used for oil paintings. It is rare for them to need any extensive cleaning, but care should be taken in framing and hanging them.

Samplers

These charming mementoes of childhood days of the Victorian era or earlier, are often framed and make admirable 'country-cottage' furnishing pieces. On the rare occasions that one might be found dirty or creased, it can be washed and ironed gently on the reverse, remembering of course that they are usually well over one hundred years old and so require careful handling.

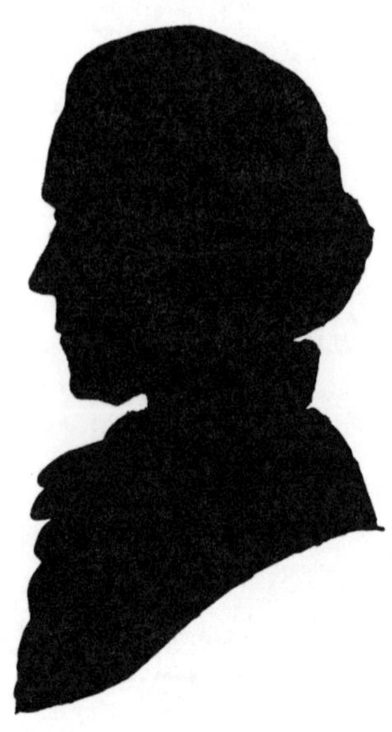

Silhouettes

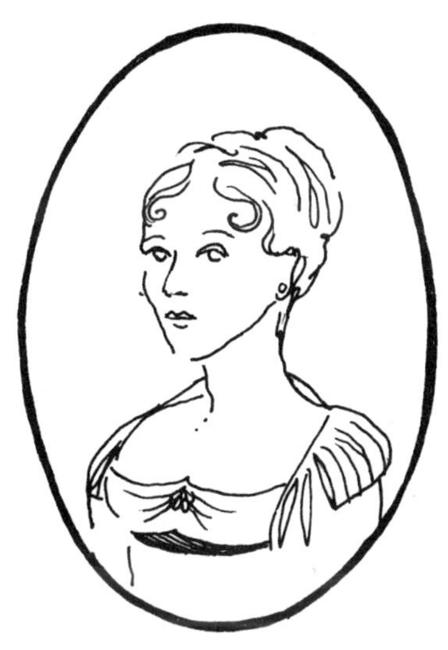

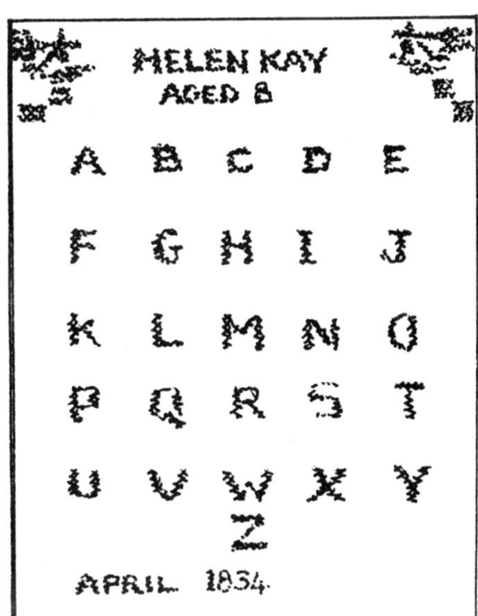

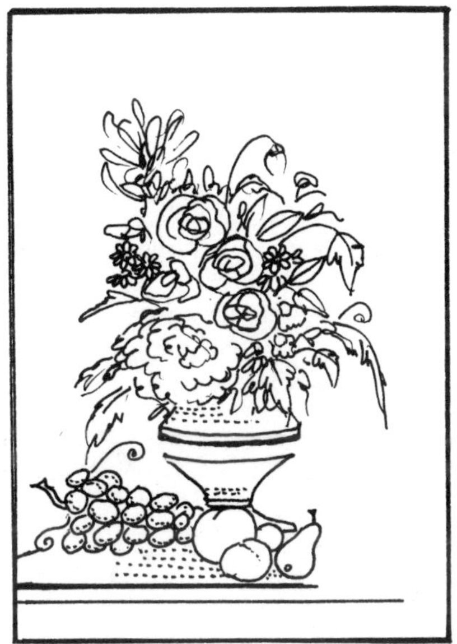

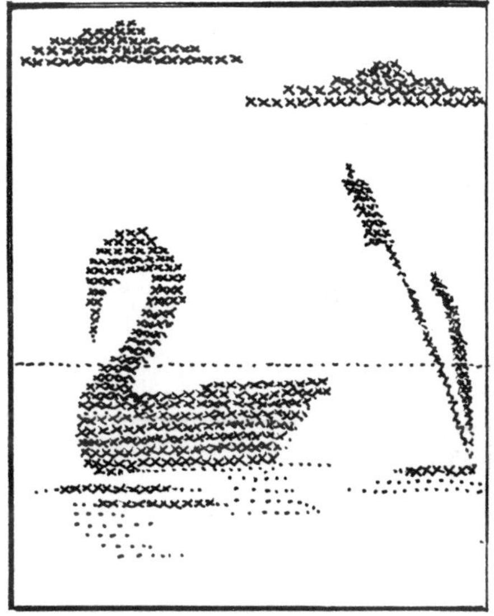

Paintings on porcelain (above) *and glass*

Samplers

Frames

Types

Generally speaking frames for oil paintings are completely different from those used for watercolours and prints. Oil-painting frames need to be much heavier and thicker to complement the picture they surround. The paintings are often well served by the ornamental decoration around the whole frame or in the corners, whereas watercolours and prints generally need a thin frame and a cardboard mount to provide a window for the painting. Watercolours and period prints always need to be framed behind glass whereas nowadays only in the case of very important or small oil paintings is glass found advisable.

Frames surrounding your pictures may be of the following types: carved frames covered in gold leaf; wooden frames having plaster cast decoration, covered in gold leaf; wooden frames painted either in a reproduction gold finish or some other colour; or frames with part plastic finishes, as with some modern ones.

It would appear that a gold finish has been most acceptable to furnishing taste as most frames incorporate it in their decoration. In fact, during the last century all exhibited paintings had to be in gold-leafed frames, often, in the case of watercolours, even having the mount rendered gold.

Of course, framing is always a matter of personal taste, but if you have a painting in its original frame you would be well advised to try to retain the original frame, not only from an aesthetically pleasing point of view, but also to maintain the value and interest of the painting. Picture dealers when viewing any picture sale automatically have their eyes drawn to paintings in their period frames. On many occasions quite important paintings have been overlooked through being disguised by a cheap, modern frame. Also of course, if you can renovate the old frame, a good deal of expense will be saved.

Removal

The removal of a picture's frame has possibly been responsible for more accidents to pictures than any other

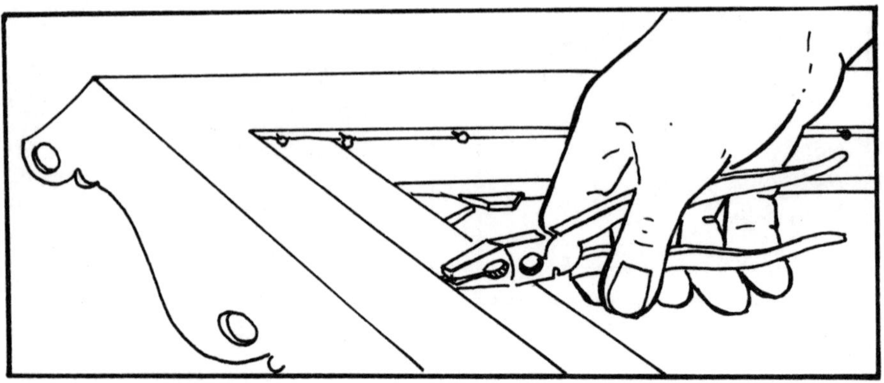

Removing a frame

single event. Even the leaning of the picture against a chair or table corner, as a preliminary to the removal, has caused many a rip or hole. So after carefully taking it down from the wall, lay the picture face down on to a clean flat table or on the floor and then, using a good pair of pliers, take out all the fixing nails or pins from the back. Only when *all* the nails have been removed and any sealing strip or paper around the edges has been removed or cut, then, with care, prise either the canvas stretcher or card out from the frame. Immediately find a safe place to store this so that no harm can come to it while in this unprotected state.

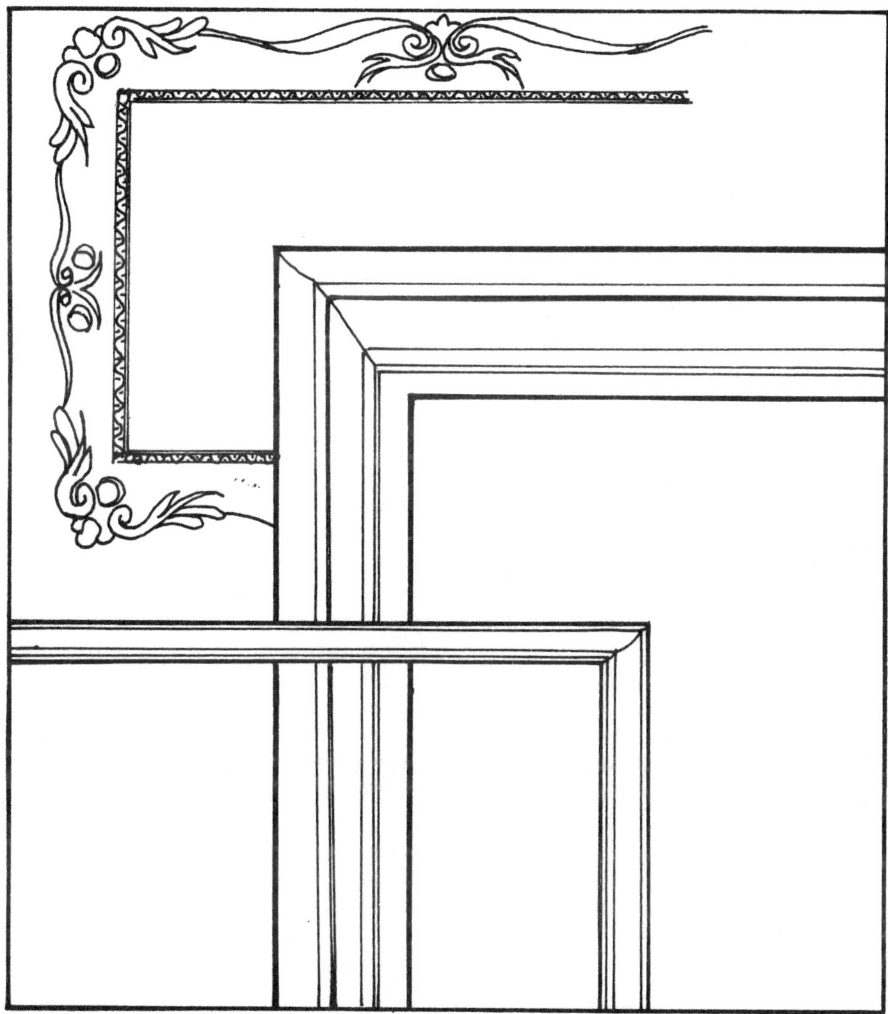

Some different types of frames

Frames

Repairing chipped gilt frames

Often after a piece of gilt has been chipped away or has been lost, its absence is revealed by the white gesso base which is left to irritate the eye. Sometimes it is sufficient to obtain a reproduction gilt paste – stocked in most art shops – and, using a brush and white spirit to dilute the paste, repaint the missing area.

If no glaring patches of white or old wood appear to break up the uniformity of the frame it is quite amazing how repainting alone will improve the appearance of many a 'tatty' frame. If the frame's beading has chipped or flaked away, and you wish to get a little more involved, you can fill the missing areas with a filler such as plastic wood, putty, or barbola paste and then, using a small piece of wood, engrave any detail or pattern of the original pieces into the soft filler. When dry, retouch the area with diluted gilt paste.

However, if faced with a more intricate or valuable frame you may wish to adopt the following professional technique.

Usually, no matter how decrepit the frame has become, there are areas of the frame which retain pieces of the original pattern, whether it be an inner beading pattern or the outer swept finish of the corners. To repair the frame successfully, it is necessary to re-mould some of the pattern to use as repair pieces.

Obtain a ball of Plasticine which will become softer when slightly warmed. Then carefully, so as not to

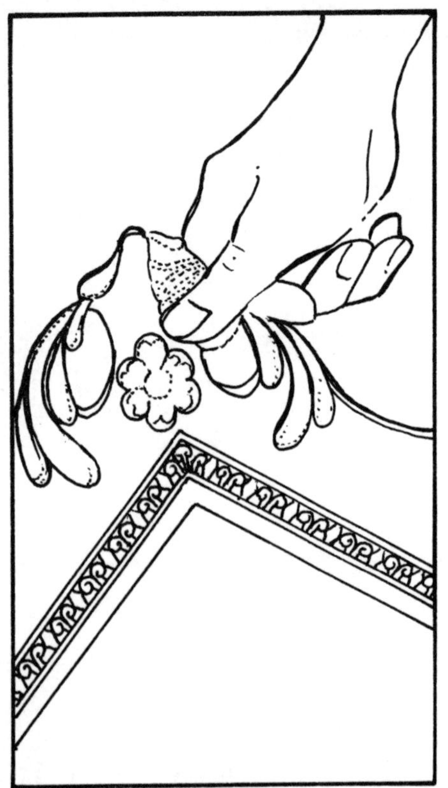

Using barbola paste to re-mould detail on a frame

cause more damage, press the Plasticine around undamaged sections, to take off a mould of the pattern. Using pieces of Plasticine to complete the mould, pour mixed plaster of Paris to the required depth. Allow plenty of time to dry, then remove from the mould and sand or cut the pieces to fit and glue into place. It may be necessary to repeat the mould many times in the event of major repairs, but as the decoration was usually made from a mould in the first place, all the parts should be re-mouldable.

After glueing into place, you may be tempted to purchase gold leaf in small book form and using red gold

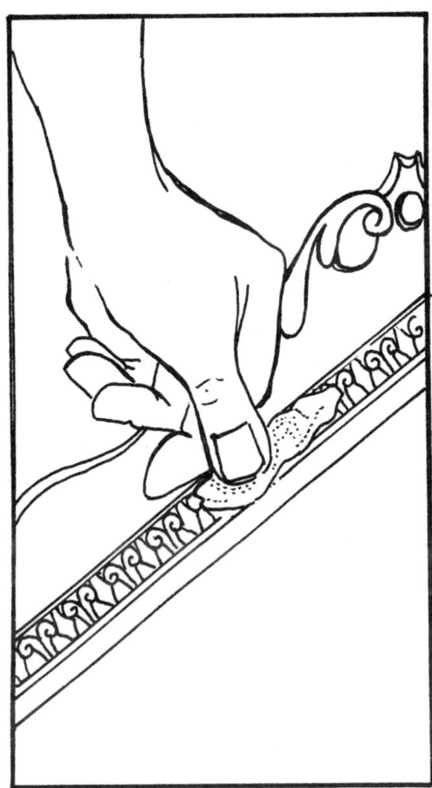

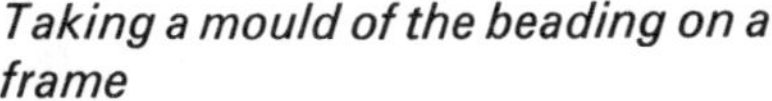

Taking a mould of the beading on a frame

size, learn the art of gilding. Speaking from experience, this is often quite unnecessary due to the fact that freshly applied gold leaf, no matter how expertly applied, looks completely out of place on a repair of an old frame, due to its new brightness. After re-gilding repairs I have had a great deal of trouble toning down the bright appearance of the new leaf. It is far simpler to paint the filler over with a red or yellow paint as a ground and then apply the gilt paste. Diluted gilt paste achieves a much closer match to the old gold and is of course much easier to apply and less expensive.

After repainting with gilt, the

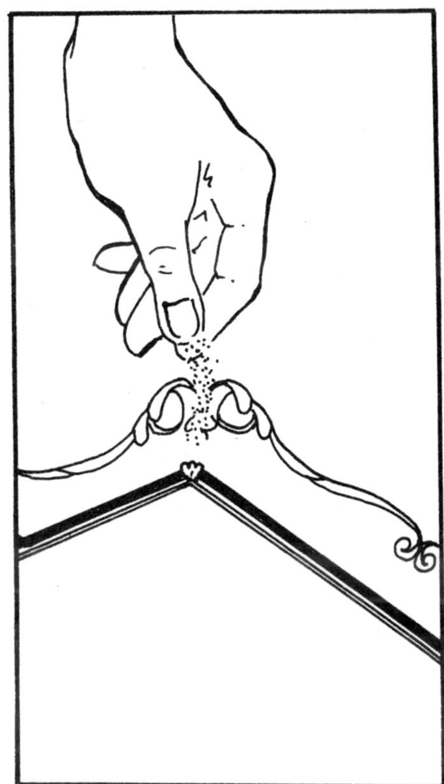

A repair can be made to look older by sprinkling it with dust

repair usually looks out of place due to its newness and here the tricks of the professional can complete the repair. Most old frames of any intricacy accumulate a patina of dust in the nooks and crannies of the design. Using a brush, apply some paper gum to these nooks and crannies, and then sprinkle on some dust obtained from a vacuum cleaner bag. After any surplus dust has been blown off, an old toothbrush with some black ink on the bristles, flicked near the frame may complete the restoration by leaving some reproduction fly spots ! This will usually finish the repair and deceive even the most experienced eye.

Frames

Brightening gold leaf

Usually if one takes warm water and a brush to a frame with gold leaf on it, some cleaning will occur, but more often the leaf is removed and a very sad rubbed frame is left. I have found that a piece of lemon rubbed lightly over the surface of the frame not only removes some of the dirt, by virtue of the texture of the lemon flesh, but also brightens the original gold leaf.

Unless in a very dirty state, the renovation of gold leaf is best restricted to the lemon treatment by the amateur renovator so that no permanent loss occurs. If it does, you can however resort to the reproduction gilt finishes, which, although coming close, never reach the luxuriance of the original leaf.

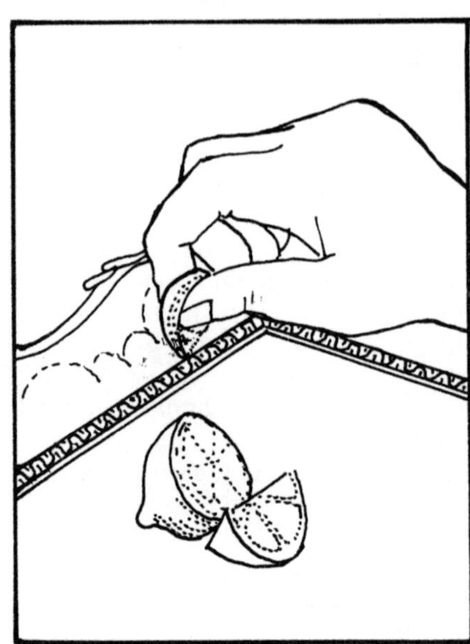

Renovation of other types of frame

Most picture framers have, over the years, accumulated stocks of old frames, often of better quality than that which now surrounds many pictures. Often you can obtain some good old frames fairly inexpensively or, if necessary, completely renovate your old frame. Even if the frame is old and looks completely decrepit, the wood may be of fair quality, and in these days of dwindling resources and high costs it may be better to attempt some 'last-ditch' renovation.

In the case of old plaster and gilt frames, these can be stripped by being immersed in hot water and abraded so that all the old gilt plaster comes away. After the application of a paint stripper, the original wood should be revealed. After drying, sanding, re-staining and waxing, one could be quite pleased with the quality of the finished frame, especially when one remembers that the frame was about to be discarded as a piece of old rubbish! It might surprise some people to know that a good many expensive and sumptuous-looking pine-frames now surrounding mirrors began their lives as gilt frames of nineteenth-century paintings.

If you are fortunate enough to own a set of pictures framed in what is known as maple veneer, then these frames – which were popular in nineteenth-century sporting circles – should always be well looked after. They rarely show any bad signs of wear and apart from the need for an occasional waxing, retain their furnishing charm to this day and are certainly unobtainable from any standard framer nowadays.

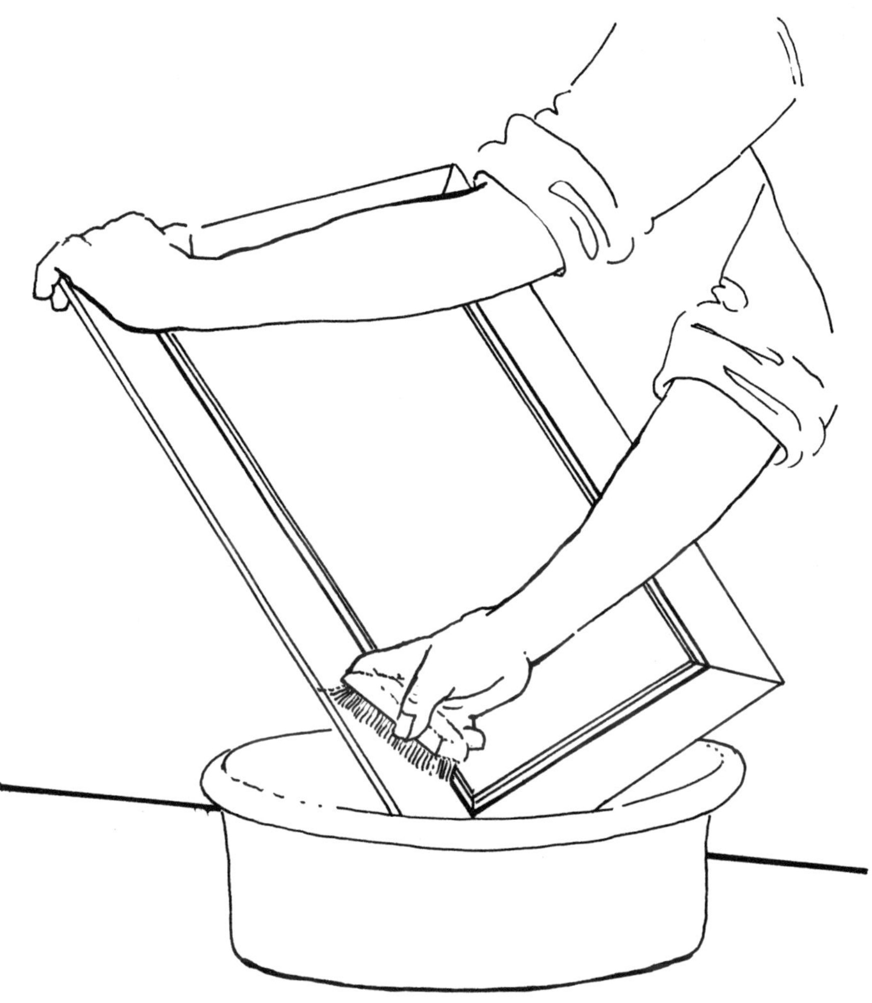

Stripping an old frame

Re-mounting prints and watercolours

In the case of watercolours and prints it is often the mount that is of prime concern to the observer. Often the mount becomes discoloured or foxed, or one just gets plain tired of it. As the mount can either make or break the appearance of the watercolour or print, great attention should be paid to its colour, decoration and size; in fact it should be considered part of the work of art itself. A common mistake made in cutting a new mount is to have an equal border all around the picture. It is now commonly recognised that to achieve a balanced effect, a greater width should be allowed along the bottom, so that the appearance is not as in (a) but as in (b).

When cutting a mount, first decide on the colour of your card, remembering that quality watercolours should really be mounted using an off-white/cream card. Of course taste varies and you may prefer a tinted colour to complement either your own furnishings, or a colour in the picture.

Measure the picture and decide the width you require for your mount, remembering the additional width to the bottom edge. By means of a simple addition you should be able to calculate the total size necessary. Cut this size out using a sharp knife and a board or old cardboard slipped underneath so that you do not find yourself cutting your new front-room carpet or table. Remember that the cutting of the mount is an exercise not to be hurried.

Using a ruler as in the illustration, you should be able to find the correct corner point. Using a sharp knife, run the blade along, using a metal ruler as a guiding edge. Either cut the card completely, or lightly score the line with the knife and ruler and then, if you have a steady hand, follow the scored cut freehand, remembering of course to maintain a steady angle of approximately 45° so that a bevelled edge is produced. Completion of the corners may present a little difficulty. It is usually found advisable not to

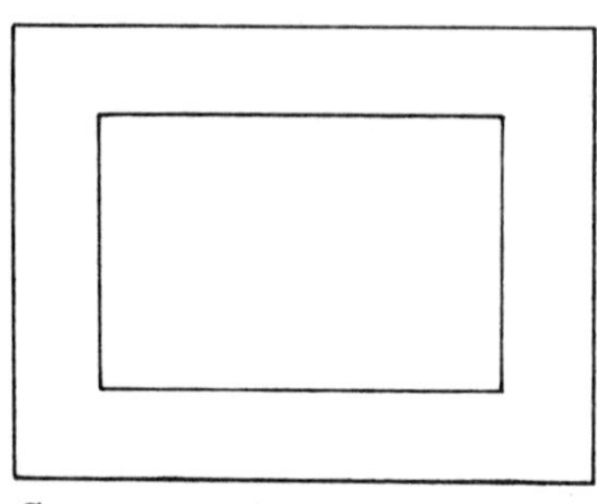

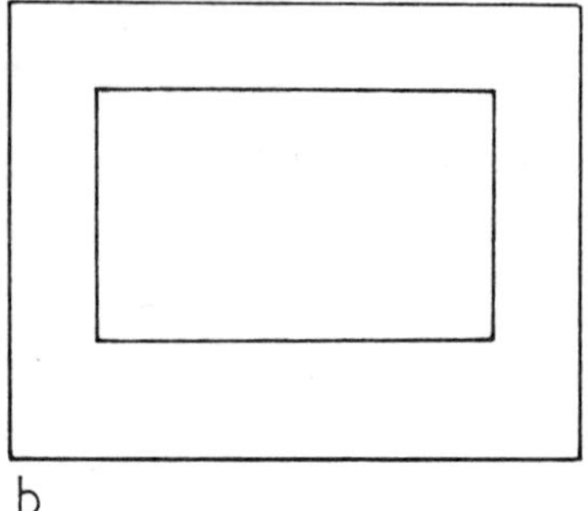

When cutting a new mount, do not leave an equal margin as in (*a*) *but allow a greater margin at the bottom as in* (*b*)

cut right to the corner, but to press the rectangle out and finish the cut with a new razor blade used carefully. It is best to practise this technique before finishing the corner on your carefully measured, almost completed mount. With a little experience a neat corner can be your reward. If you do not use this technique, you must exercise great care when getting near the corner so that the cut does not extend too far.

After the cutting of the mount has been completed, you may wish to aid the presentation of the finished picture by drawing lines around the cut-out window and adding a wash. This is usually termed as a line and wash and is generally of the type shown in the illustration.

A watercolour wash is chosen to complement the colour scheme of the picture, this wash being always very diluted and not in a strong colour. In order to prevent a hard edge forming in the painted wash when you paint back to the beginning, some framers first put on a wash in clear water. This has the effect of helping to achieve an even wash of colour as you join back to the beginning, when doing the actual watercolour wash.

The lines should be drawn using either a lining pen and watercolour, or a watercolour felt-tip. If you apply the lines after painting the wash the lines follow the edges of the wash, finishing it in a neat fashion. Sometimes a thin strip of gold paper can make the line-finish even more effective.

Another way of achieving an excellent renovation in the event of an old stained mount is to cut another mount with a window just slightly larger than the old mount. This, when placed over the old mount, will achieve an effect of even greater depth and will cover over any staining or discoloration on the face of the old mount.

To facilitate measuring, it is sufficient to draw around the old mount and, whilst keeping it very still, press a pin through where you wish the inner corners of the new mount to be.

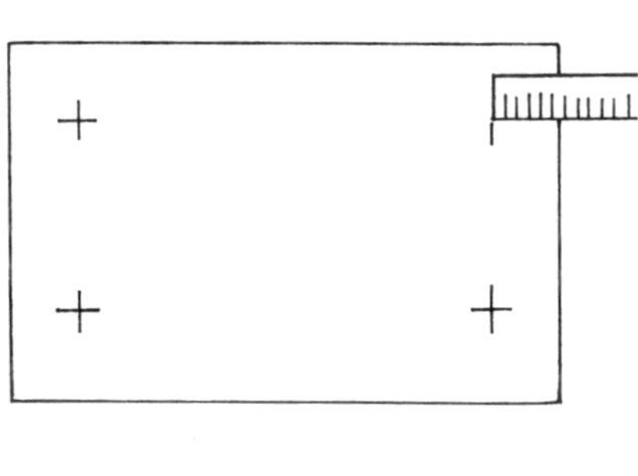

Method of finding the corners

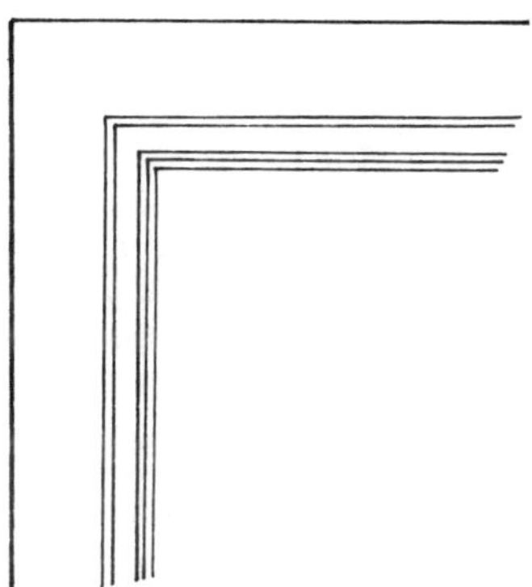

A typical mount decoration

Replacing glass

Old glass often becomes dirty and discoloured by nicotine, fly spots and so on. You can clean it with warm soapy water, but take great care when handling it as it can become more brittle with age. Some old glass, when viewed from the side, gives a wavy appearance due to imperfections in its manufacture, and you may like to get a new piece of glass cut.

When choosing glass, do not forget to tell the glazier that it is for a picture or, better still, give him the frame to cut the glass to size, and then he will be sure to use picture glass which is thinner than standard window glass. A modern introduction into the glazing world has been non-reflective glass. It is occasionally used for framing purposes, but does tend to give a slightly misty appearance to the picture.

To achieve a remarkably clear, clean glass both on the inside and outside, you will find that a rag moistened with methylated spirit will produce a streak-free, grease-free shining surface with no finger prints visible on the glass when the framing is completed, even when viewed from the side.

Finally when replacing glass, whether cutting it yourself or merely transporting it, take great care in handling the edges so as to avoid accidents.

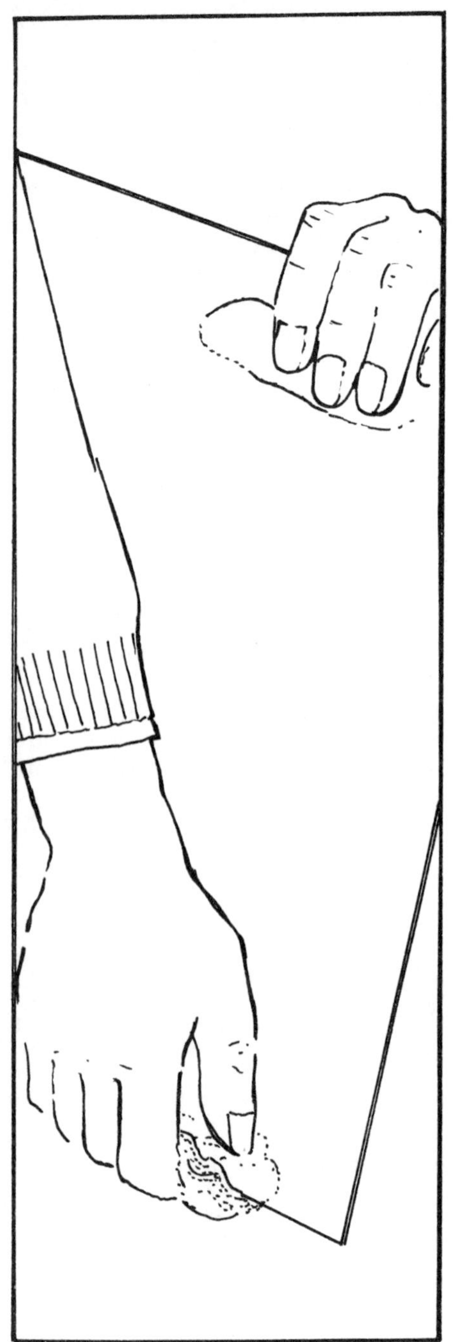

Handle glass with care

Conclusion

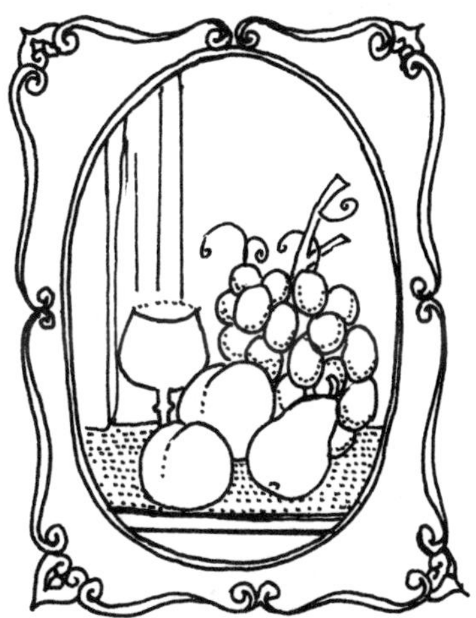

Remember that although this book explains many useful techniques, it cannot replace experience and 'the feel' of what looks right or is necessary. Further, to anyone trying a new craft for the first time, remember that practise is one of the greatest of teachers, and if you are considering the renovation of a painting or print of value, do not be afraid to consult an expert in the field. If the restoration is to be carried out by a professional obtain several opinions and estimates.

Of course, prevention is always better than cure – so take every care over choosing where you display or store paintings or prints. They should be kept in a safe and airy place, away from direct sunlight and extremes of temperature. Your paintings and prints will then continue to give pleasure to the present generation and provide modest heirlooms for the future.

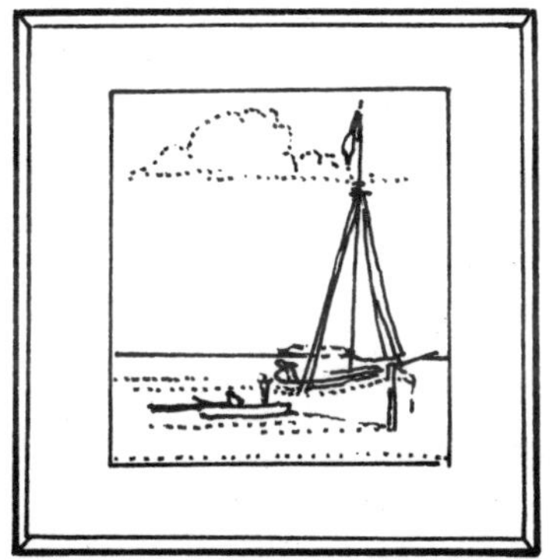

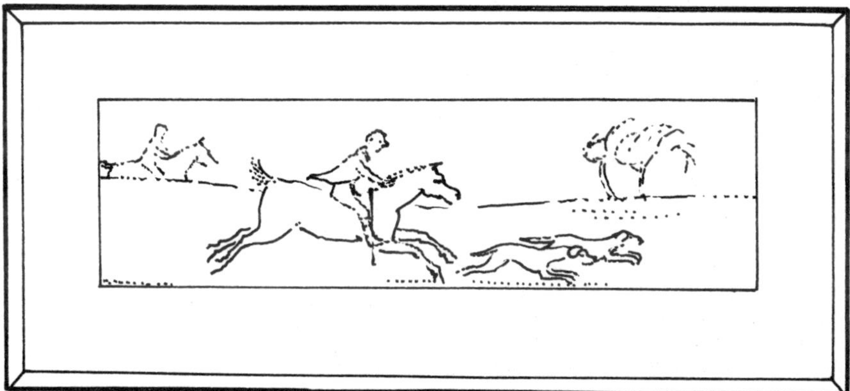

Glossary

Acetone A colourless, organic solvent with a characteristic odour. Dissolves varnish films and some paints. Highly inflammable

Ammonia Valuable cleansing agent, usually obtained as a 10 per cent solution in water

Beeswax Obtainable either in natural yellow-brown, or white fine grade. Melting point is *c* 65°C

Benzene Solvent for oily deposits. Highly inflammable

Bloom A cloudy appearance sometimes seen on the varnish of oil paintings. Probably due to the presence of moisture

Brushes For oil painting, bristle, sable or similar. For watercolour painting, sable

Carbon tetrachloride Excellent solvent for grease and oil-based dirt. Fumes can be injurious

Chlorine A gas often produced in bleaching reactions. The fumes should be avoided

Engraving Engraving is usually performed on a metal plate. The inked impression of an engraved plate on paper is referred to as an engraving. Mezzotint and dry point are forms of engraving

Etching Similar process to engraving but the design is etched into a copper plate by means of acid

Fly spots These are due to deposits left by the common house fly

Gesso Ground chalk mixed with glue or gelatin as a binder. Used as a ground for painting on to bare canvas or wood

Gum Gum arabic in solution has adhesive properties and is sometimes used as a medium for watercolours

Megilp A mixture of oils, wax and varnish. Sometimes used in the eighteenth and nineteenth centuries as a painting medium

Oil paints These are composed not only of pigment but also a base, a medium such as linseed oil and other constituents to promote satisfactory drying and handling

Pastels A crayon made from pigment and fine chalk and bound with gum

Silver fish An insect that causes considerable damage due to its liking for sized paper. Fumigation with carbon disulphide is effective

Thymol An antiseptic of the phenol group. A valuable fungicide

Vellum Finely prepared skin of sheep, goat or calf. Used for miniature painting or illuminated texts

Illustrated by the author

British Library Cataloguing in Publication Data
Cook, Ian
Renovating prints, paintings and frames.
– (Penny pinchers).
1. Painting – Conservation and restoration
I. Title II. Series
751.6 ND1650

ISBN 0 7153 7870 8

Set in 9D on 11 pt. Univers
and printed in Great Britain
by Redwood Burn Limited
Trowbridge & Esher
for David & Charles (Publishers) Limited
Brunel House Newton Abbot Devon